The Falcons

The
Falcons

by

Nicholas J. Everett

PUBLISHERS

ROBERT HALE · LONDON

© *Nicholas J. Everett 1978*
First published in Great Britain 1978

ISBN 0 7091 6908 6

Robert Hale Limited
Clerkenwell House
Clerkenwell Green
London, EC1

Photoset By Ebenezer Baylis & Son Ltd, Worcester, & London.
Printed and bound in Great Britain by
Weatherby Woolnough, Northants.

Contents

Illustrations

Picture Credits
Ministry of Defence, 1, 6, 7, 12, 14, 15, 17, 21, 22; Sergeant C. F. E. Smedley, 2, 4; Author, 3, 8, 9, 23, 24, 25, 26, 27, 28, 29, 30, 31, 32, 33, 34, 37, 38, 42, 44; Ken George, 5, 35; Sergeant G. Pierce, 10, 16, 18, 19, 20; Steve Rowe, 11; Flight Sergeant A. Betteridge, 13; Roger Tamblyn (Essex County Newspapers), 36, 39, 40, 41, 43.

Acknowledgements

My thanks are due to Graham Pierce who is responsible for many of the free-fall photographs in this book and provided me with them.

The writing of the book was made possible by the co-operation of a number of people who for six months welcomed me into their midst even though I was a complete stranger and even though it was not always perfectly convenient. For that I thank them.

Thanks also to those at the Ministry of Defence who went to some lengths to make arrangements and obtain necessary clearances for me to fly on display and practice drops.

A number of the photographs included in the book are reproduced by permission of Sergeant 'Oscar' Smedley (R.A.F.), Rodger Tamblyn of the *Colchester Evening Gazette* and Tony Betteridge (Flt-Lt — R.A.F.). My thanks to them.

Finally, I would like to thank Wing Commander White, Squadron Leader Haggart and Flight-Lieutenant Bales for giving the project their approval in the first place and allowing me to be a fly on the Falcons' wall for six months.

To my delightful children
and to
the special things which bring a little magic
into people's lives

Introduction

Faced with the prospect of launching himself out of an aeroplane flying two miles above the ground, to plummet earthward for a minute or more at speeds in excess of 120 m.p.h., the average man in the street would probably feel distinctly ill. Very likely, he would be almost paralysed with fear. The feat is, after all, perhaps beyond the physical and mental capacities of all but a relatively few highly skilled individuals who are sufficiently motivated to master an activity which is amongst the most alien to sport generally.

This book concerns a small group of individuals who almost routinely, as a part of their everyday working lives, perform such spectacular and hair-raising feats for the benefit of enraptured audiences the world over.

Perhaps individuals is the wrong word to use since they are essentially a team that demonstrates teamwork and professional expertise, in dazzling fashion.

They are the Falcons, the Royal Air Force's world famous free-fall parachute display team who each year delight hundreds of thousands of spectators at air displays all over the world. Their colourful parachute canopies and smoke trails are a familiar sight at international air shows, R.A.F. open days and civilian and military shows both at home and abroad; they form, together with the equally famous Red Arrows Aerobatic Team, the major showpiece of the Royal Air Force.

The motto of the Parachute Training School at Brize Norton in Oxfordshire asserts that "Knowledge Dispels Fear", an appropriate enough slogan since, as parachuting instructors first and foremost at the school, they are dealing with an

11

activity which has perhaps a greater fear element than any other. The motto is clearly borne out each time they jump and this book sets out to take a behind-the-scenes look at how this knowledge is acquired and the way in which it is applied to the Falcons' displays to make them the unique attraction that they are.

Those thousands of entranced spectators must frequently ask themselves as they watch the twelve doll-like figures hurtling towards the ground — "I wonder what it is really like to do that?". In the course of this book, I hope to answer that question.

The Falcons were known originally as 'The Big Six' at a time when the team was half its present size. That is going back to 1961 when sky-diving was really only beginning to establish itself as a sport in this country and was somewhat less sophisticated than it is today.

In those days, the team would jump from a Beverley or Hastings aircraft at more or less today's heights but the ensuing aerial manoeuvres were rather less intricate than they are now. The years of experience have lent an unprecedented precision and synchronisation to the Falcons' displays, a result of the constant development of equipment, techniques and ideas. To anyone who has seen the displays, it is immediately apparent why the team is so named, such is the swiftness, grace and artistry of their one-minute 'flight' prior to deploying their parachutes.

Entertainment alone, however, is only partly the objective of their work, since, as instructors at Brize Norton, their primary concern is the training of parachutists in all arms of the services, and the passing on of their knowledge to men who in some cases have never even sat inside an aeroplane. The team's secondary role as entertainers must surely help to inspire many 'green' and apprehensive pupils with the knowledge that they are in highly skilled hands, and with the self-confidence so essential to their trade.

One most significant side effect of the Falcons' displays and the preparation and practice that goes into them is the wealth of new knowledge that is gained. Like experts in any sphere, sporting or otherwise, they are constantly learning, and the results of their world-wide experience of parachuting are frequently of significance in the modification and improvement of today's military parachuting techniques. This in itself is a sizeable responsibility since military parachutists (i.e. parachute soldiers) are by sheer weight of numbers the largest single factor in the parachuting field in this country.

Since the beginning of the Second World War when the first Parachute Training School was established at Ringway in Manchester, airborne troops have completed more than one million 'static-line' parachute descents. This is a method used by troops and novice parachutists that differs from free-fall parachuting in that the parachute is opened automatically, by a line attached to the plane, as soon as its wearer leaves the aircraft.

The end of the war saw the transfer of the school to Upper Heyford and thence, in 1950, to Abingdon in Berkshire which remained 'Number One PTS' until 1976.

Now based at Brize Norton, the Falcons continue to apply their knowledge and skills to the training of Services' parachutists, many of whom have the chance to sample the exhilaration of sport parachuting at moderate cost. Significantly, not a great percentage avail themselves of the opportunity, possibly an indication of the degree of mental stress sometimes involved.

Although still something of a minority sport so far as actual numbers of participants is concerned, sky-diving is fast becoming an extremely popular spectator sport, thanks largely to the dozens of air shows each summer and the accompanying display drops by a handful of teams and particularly by the Falcons. Perhaps the day is not too far away when turnstiles click as crowds throng to sky-diving displays and competitions as they at present throng to cricket and football matches, for there is no doubt that many of the public find the activity a source of some wonder and amusement. Perhaps that is because, for the great majority, actual participation in the sport can only be a flight of fancy. One would not attempt to hazard a guess at the percentage of the population who possess the necessary mental and physical attributes to cope with an activity that is alien to all one's instincts, but one would not imagine that percentage to be a large one. That is probably why the sport has an aura of fascination for its spectators, since for most of them it is one that is totally removed from anything they have ever experienced or indeed would ever wish to experience. Be that as it may, I hope the contents of this book at least begin to convey some of the irresistible impact the sport can have. It is perhaps not unlike the effect that motor racing can have on a Grand Prix driver, an effect described rather cleverly by film star and racing driver in his own right, Steve McQueen in the film *Grand Prix*. To him, the tension and drama of the big race is ". . . Living; everything else is just waiting".

ONE

'Bomb-Burst'!

Imagine yourself, if you can, in the belly of a huge Hercules transport aircraft 12,000 feet above the ground. The noise from the four, awesomely powerful engines drowns all ordinary conversation as the craft closes steadily with its target dropping zone two miles below. There, tens of thousands of spectators gaze expectantly up into the blue, hoping to catch a first glimpse of the Falcons' aircraft as it approaches.

Inside the Hercules, the twelve-man team sits composed on the inward-facing seats, making last-minute checks of equipment, perhaps going through a mental rehearsal of their performance. Without exception, they are feeling the tension in the guts that most, top, professional sportsmen feel prior to any testing event. (A surprisingly good thing, this, since it is a sign that the body's 'fright, flight or fight' mechanism is preparing the whole body system for a period of intense activity.)

To a man, the team can feel the adrenalin pumping into their bloodstreams, ensuring that brain and muscle are operating at peak efficiency.

Just a couple of minutes to go and there is a final, all-round check of the most vital equipment — helmet, goggles, main parachute at the back, and the reserve 'chute at the front (which incidentally is a convenient seating for the all-important altimeter and stop-watch), smoke canisters secure to the ankles and ripcord free of obstruction (rather important, this!). Thumbs up all round and the doors are opened to reveal white wisps of cloud whipping by and a breathtakingly spectacular view of green countryside far below the aircraft.

15

It is at this point that the average man (and who can blame him) may just feel something deep within his soul telling him to stay exactly where he is; but then this book can hardly be said to be about the average man. For the scream of the slipstream which accompanies the removal of the plane's port and starboard doors is the signal for the occupants to stand up, move to their positions near the doors, await the preparatory warning light there and moments later the 'exit' signal from the team leader, now kneeling in the door watching the target gliding by two miles below. (Use is also sometimes made of the rear tailgate ramp which drops down for a team exit.)

Meanwhile, down on the dropping zone, tens of thousands of pairs of eyes scan the heavens and focus on the Hercules almost directly above from which the twelve are due to emerge at any moment. In the aircraft with only seconds left and nods all round, everyone is ready to go. All eyes on the team leader, he suddenly stands to face the team, up goes his thumb and within a frantic and climactic five seconds, all twelve jumpers step forward and launch themselves out of the aircraft and into a buffeting and deafening slipstream. They fall clear of that within a very few seconds, and quickly accelerate to 120 m p.h., their fall traced by plumes of coloured smoke playing out behind them. These same smoke trails are particularly effective in demonstrating the Falcons' movement across the sky ('tracking' they call it). This is achieved by bringing the arms into the sides soon after leaving the aircraft, and bringing the extended legs together much in the shape of a dart or 'delta' position. This has the effect of producing a downward speed of nearer 180 m.p.h. but at the same time a horizontal speed of about 70 m.p.h. This manoeuvre is, of course, essential to the Falcons' main display showpiece known as the 'bomb-burst' which they initiate soon after leaving the slipstream.

Those on the dropping zone see a combined team manoeuvre of near perfect symmetry. A central core of four or six men (the first ones out) link up in the sky and fall vertically in a stable 'frog' position (arms and legs spread wide, face

towards the ground). This helps to prevent the turning and
unbalancing tendencies of the rush of air, especially after terminal velocity has been reached. This is quite simply the speed
at which a falling body stops accelerating due to the force of
air resistance, a speed attained after ten to twelve seconds
when the parachutist in the basic frog position will be
travelling at about 120 m.p.h.

Whilst the link-up men are thus employed, the remaining
eight begin to move across the sky at forty-five degree intervals
five seconds after leaving the aircraft. It is this that creates the
spectacular and famous bomb-burst effect as the red, white
and blue smoke trails scythe symmetrically outwards for twenty-
five seconds. The trackers then turn and trace an identical
pattern for a further twenty-five seconds in the opposite direction until they reach their opening heights of between 3,000
and 2,000 feet.

Meanwhile, the link-men break at 5,000 feet and they in
turn bomb-burst outwards to their opening point where they
'flare out' for minimum speed ready for the pull at 2,000 feet.

The whole rather complicated procedure is so perfectly
timed that on its completion all twelve Falcons' parachutes
open at prearranged heights simultaneously and in an
organised group rather than scattered at random in the sky.

It then remains only for them to steer into their targets with
the unerring accuracy that generally accompanies their performances and this particularly colourful operation takes two
to three minutes under normal circumstances. The reason for
the differing opening heights is to prevent the whole team
coming into the target *en masse* which would pose problems of
congestion and possible collision.

Such displays are naturally dependent on weather conditions being suitable. Ideally, a cloudless sky below 12,000
feet is necessary from the point of view of both spectators and
jumpers, and whilst a breeze is no problem, wind of any great
strength is frequently the major threat to a display. In fact, the
pilot of the Hercules may well overfly the target by a mile or

more before the team leader gives the signal for exit, in order to allow for the 'drift' that parachutists are subject to.

Regardless of wind strength, however, the team always have to contend with wind of a different sort — the potentially terrifying slipstream which attacks at 120 knots as soon as they set foot outside the aircraft. This can be both a problem and a blessing, since although a violent slipstream can make any parachutist tumble, somersault or turn against his will, it also gives him air resistance to work against immediately he is out of the aircraft, thus enabling him to initiate horizontal movement sooner than if there were no slipstream. If he were jumping from a static point such as a balloon, he would need to fall for several seconds before he had built up enough air resistance to work against, which would effectively reduce, for example, tracking time in a descent. So the Falcons use the slipstream to their advantage by presenting their bodies to it symmetrically. If by chance an arm or leg does go out of place and control is lost, each member of the team can right himself (that is turn to fall face down) from any position in the sky.

In the event of a cloud base between 7,000 and 5,000 feet, the usual display is the 'clover leaf'. The team exit as for the bomb-burst, the first four linking together whilst the trackers move symmetrically outwards prior to completing an into-the-wind track turn, making for their opening points of 3,000 and 2,500 feet. The four link men break off at 4,000 feet and themselves track out to their opening point at 2,000 feet.

If conditions are even more unfavourable with cloud base between 5,000 and 2,500 feet, the 'stack pull' is demonstrated. This jump entails a team exit hard on each others' heels and an immediate outward turn at ninety degrees to aircraft heading. The ensuing fall is in the normal frog position (in other words no tracking takes place) whilst all eyes are careful to note when the lowest man's canopy begins to deploy. This man is of course the first to exit the aircraft and he pulls at 2,000 feet. The effect of the remainder of the team opening their 'chutes at the same time as the lowest man, is to stagger the team at safe intervals in the sky from 2,000 to 3,000 feet just as in the bomb-burst. They are then free to concentrate on steering into the impact point.

During the free-fall period in the stack pull, the team do not watch the lowest man to the exclusion of all else. It would not be impossible for him to be late in his opening for some reason, which in turn would make the rest of the team late and throw out their timing. They therefore occasionally refer to their own altimeters and stop-watches and in that way can always keep stock of their own situation.

Because they are performing descents such as those above, the Falcons are also committed to and proficient in 'relative' work; that is when two or more jumpers work together in the sky during free fall, possibly linking hands to form a circle, or performing manoeuvres around each other. Obviously, to succeed in this, the last man out of the aircraft must have a means of catching up with the first who may already have been falling for four or five seconds when the last man makes his exit. How is this achieved? As was mentioned earlier, a skilled free-fall artist is able to control his rate of descent within certain limits. The first man out of the aircraft therefore aims to fall as slowly as possible, the slowest he can hope to achieve being the 120 m.p.h. attained by presenting as large a body surface area as possible to the air. (If you have ever put your hand out of the window of a speeding car, you will have felt the varying resistances that can be obtained by inclining the hand at different angles.)

The first man to exit, therefore, adopts a basic, stable position, arms and legs spread wide and face towards the ground, since the canopy must be free to deploy cleanly from the back. This minimises the risk of the parachutist rolling over into the rigging lines as they deploy, a potential cause of a malfunction.

Whilst the first man is thus falling 'slowly', the last may be falling as much as 50 or 60 m.p.h. faster. This he achieves by streamlining his body position, bending arms and legs and bringing them in close to the body, known in the jump world as 'working small'. Alternatively, he can obtain the maximum downward speed by going into a 'max track' where the legs are brought together and arms into the sides with the hands at thigh level. This causes a curious, head-down position and permits movement across the sky. The 'chaser' is therefore in a position to place himself above, below or level with a partner or group and it is this that makes possible such self-explanatory formations as 'four in line' or 'duet' or, most spectacular of all, the complete circles involving six or eight or more of the team.

This sort of work is really only suitable for the higher jumps around 12,000 feet which give the team a full minute of free fall to play with. Even then, there is little margin for error since manoeuvres must be swift and precise if the desired link is to be achieved. When they are hurtling towards the ground at 120 m.p.h. plus, they have little time to correct mistakes. In that respect, this sort of relative work is a means of perfecting both team co-operation and individual skill and control in the air.

Predictably, the Falcons' equipment is of a specialised nature and chosen with functional efficiency as the highest priority. The team are confident that whilst few items of equipment can be termed 'infallible', theirs is particularly reliable. Their record of no malfunctions in the last three years is testimony to that, although they would never dream of jumping without the reserve parachute of course.

By far the largest piece of equipment essential to the Falcons' needs is their vehicle to the jump height two miles up, and in some cases considerably in excess of that. Their Hercules aircraft is designed primarily as a long range transporter of small military vehicles and of military parachutists in full combat gear. It is capable of carrying sixty-two paratroopers whose main parachutes are attached to the aircraft by means of a static line which opens the 'chute automatically as soon as its wearer leaves the plane via doors on the port and starboard sides of the fuselage. The Falcons in their free-fall role, however, have the alternative of jumping from the tailgate ramp beneath the tail of the plane.

Less well known as Falcon carriers are the Wessex and Puma helicopters from whose side doors the team make their exits. On helicopter descents, jumpers learn to fall well away from the downdraught produced by the rotor blades before operating their ripcords. An early pull a second or two after leaving the helicopter could cause a collapsed canopy as a result of downward buffeting of air on to the canopy.

The parachute itself was until 1978 the well tried and tested, American-designed Para-Commander which first appeared in the 1960s. Parachute designers have since introduced a number of novel shapes into the parachuting world but more of that later. In the past, the manoeuvrability and reliability of the 'P.C.' has proved most suitable for large team displays. Its design gives it certain lift characteristics, much in the fashion of a non-rigid glider, whilst its spectacular controllability is made possible by slots cut out of the rear of the canopy. These also give the device the familiar, tattered, full of holes appearance that is recognised at air shows the world over.

There are five stabilising panels attached to the edges or periphery of each side of the canopy. These serve to damp down undesirable oscillation which can cause the canopy to spill precious air resulting in a sudden and alarming loss of height. If this were to happen close to the ground, the landing could be anything between uncomfortable and disastrous.

Left to its own devices in still air, the P.C. has a forward speed of 10 to 12 m.p.h. which has been achieved by cutting back the leading edge of the canopy to reduce drag. Lines attached to the centre of the canopy pull down or invert the apex much in the shape of an umbrella blown inside out. This has the effect of increasing the high pressure area there and rendering the parachute more aerodynamically efficient, an important factor when it comes to performing the turns and changes in horizontal and vertical speed so essential in the approach to the target. The steering lines which control the approach terminate at two toggles held by the parachutist which he plays up and down to open or close the four turn and drive slots mentioned earlier. Without the use of these controls, the Para-Commander descends at about thirteen feet per second, but just prior to landing the 'brakes' can be applied by pulling down on both toggles, which helps to kill excess forward speed. It is this lack of forward speed which makes the Falcons so consistent in their stand-up landings and explains why they turn into the wind to land rather than run before it. (This, incidentally, is quite unlike the parachute soldier's landing which is more of a roll since he does not have the means to control his horizontal speed to the same extent.)

Naturally, every conceivable precaution goes into the packing of both main and reserve parachutes. This can be a complicated and bewildering task to the uninitiated but all the Falcons are fully qualified packers of their own parachutes. Even so, the team has a safety officer and survival equipment fitter who ensures canopies are thoroughly inspected after each descent and stringent safety measures adhered to. Given proper packing facilities, (normally a table the length of the 'chute), each of the team can pack comfortably in ten minutes.

If one were to watch the same parachute being deployed or were to see a slow-motion film of the P.C. immediately after the ripcord had been pulled, one would see, first of all, two secondary, relatively tiny drogues spring from the back-pack as the latter was split open. These are known as the extractor 'chutes, the airflow against which is responsible for pulling out the main canopy and rigging lines. If there are problems on a jump, they can happen here—there is an awful lot of nylon and rigging line packed tightly into a small space and entanglement is by no means out of the question. It is, however, unusual for the P.C. to malfunction. If a malfunction should occur, the chances of the same thing happening to the reserve must be rather remote.

Naturally, there is an emergency procedure should the main canopy fail to deploy satisfactorily. The parachutist releases himself from the delinquent parachute by means of 'capewells', (a clip arrangement) situated on the shoulder of his harness. He can then cutaway back into free fall until clear of the troublesome canopy, at which point he employs his reserve.

This is partly the reason why the parachuting powers that be, military and civilian, enforce an obligatory minimum opening height of 2,000 feet. Such a height gives reasonable time to take appropriate action should a jump not go according to plan. Not infrequently, there are twists in the rigging lines, for example, immediately after opening. It may take some seconds for the parachutist to kick and rotate himself out of these twists, and height and therefore valuable time are lost before proper canopy control is established.

One often hears the question, "But what happens if your reserve fouls up as well?". Presumably, most parachutists prefer not to think about that since, of course, if both parachutes fail completely, then an untimely end is almost inevitable, although there are occasionally miracle escapes from near-certain death under such circumstances.

A Second World War Lancaster airman chose to leave his doomed aircraft at 10,000 feet rather than perish in a blazing fuselage in which the parachutes had been incinerated. Reports, which were officially confirmed, showed that he had fallen into fir trees and thence into a bank of dense snow. Shortly afterwards, he was none the worse for his experience other than that he was a prisoner at the hands of incredulous Germans.

There are other occasions when parachutists have landed under partly functioning canopies without coming to grief. The two most common malfunctions are the 'blown periphery' and 'Roman candle'. In the former, one or more of the rigging lines can get thrown over the canopy and effectively turn it into two smaller canopies, spilling a large amount of air as it does so (a situation commonly termed a line-over). This can cause a major or minor increase in the rate of descent depending on the severity of the parachute's deformation.

The Roman candle effect can be more alarming still. In this case, air never manages to fill the canopy properly and it therefore fails to develop its proper umbrella shape. It looks almost as if the neck of the parachute is being kept closed by a draw-string and the canopy takes on a longitudinal appearance. That is serious and nearly always necessitates use of the reserve since that sort of shape must greatly increase the rate of fall.

Nowadays, these sort of incidents are comparatively rare. In fact, parachuting is statistically safer than many sports in terms of fatalities and injuries. Even were it not, there is little point in approaching a sport which has an element of risk attached with the question "But what happens if . . .?" As the Falcons have faith in their proven equipment so a Grand Prix driver must believe his machine will not let him down approaching a corner at 100 m.p.h. or more. Or a Test batsman must believe he can keep his temple clear of a 90 m.p.h. bouncer, or a scrum-half must believe he can protect his skull from flying boots whenever he falls on the ball in front of a pack of ravaging forwards or . . . the list is endless. Suffice it to say that the sport is more risky than some but less risky than most — thanks mainly to strict rules concerning procedures, training, learning and equipment. These stringent measures stretch even to the point of deliberately staging an emergency situation (for example the 'cutaway') both as an entertaining spectacle and as practice in the unlikely event of it actually being employed 'in anger'. Needless to say, when a parachutist does intend to perform the cutaway technique, he generally wears a third parachute, since he knows he will be employing his reserve and therefore needs a standby should that fail. In other words, he always aims to have a follow-up to his primary means of descent. (Incidentally, there is on film a sequence shot some years ago of American stunt man Rod Pack, who left a light airplane more than two miles above the ground wearing no parachute at all. For a fee of some £40,000 he then free fell for a minute or so and manoeuvred himself into a position which enabled him to clip on a parachute handed to him by a fellow parachutist who jumped several seconds after Pack's exit. That of course is making parachuting more hazardous than it need be. Pack himself never repeated this most daring of stunts. He was, after all, going against all the rules of self-preservation and one cannot expect to remain healthy for very long if one makes a habit of doing that.)

No doubt the Falcons' long record of trouble-free descents is due largely to their observance of these same rules which minimise the possibility of something totally unexpected happening. There is, however, no guarantee of safety in parachuting; the unexpected is frequently just around the corner. An incident that springs to mind is the two-minute freefall from 25,000 feet of *Blue Peter*'s John Noakes. A relatively inexperienced parachutist, Noakes was prepared for his mind-blowing feat by the Falcons in a matter of weeks and in the event proved more than equal to the task.

Whilst giving a running commentary on his impressions and feelings as he fell, he quite suddenly and alarmingly was flipped over on to his back as the Falcons teamed up in a circle about him. He was for some seconds quite out of control, a daunting experience for a novice parachutist, yet he continued without panic to explain his demise as he hurtled toward the ground on his back. A pretty cool customer. Fortunately, the Falcons on each side of him managed to help him turn right side up.

Thinking his most anxious moments were behind him (or rather above him) he pulled his ripcord at the required height and to his horror found that nothing very much happened for a few seconds. The sudden jerk of the deploying canopy was a long time coming, a heart-stopping moment even for experienced parachutists. His falling body had left behind it an area of low pressure, almost a vacuum, at the point where the previously mentioned extractor 'chutes should have filled with air, thence to drag out the main canopy. The extractors were consequently bobbing about uselessly for a short time although it did not seem such a short time to John Noakes. Such 'burbles', as they are known, or 'hesitations', are not unusual and normally last only two or three seconds before the extractors catch enough air to do their job. If this is not the case, the parachutist has only to wriggle an arm or shoulder to alter his slipstream effect; this happened in John Noakes' case and all was well.

The chances are that future Falcons' displays will be performed with the revolutionary Cloud-type parachute. Shaped almost like a flat, rectangular wing, the Cloud is even more of a non-rigid glider than the P.C. in that its remarkably aerodynamic properties give a parachutist enormous powers of control over his rate of descent and forward speed. Almost completely gone is the familiar umbrella or inverted saucer shape of the conventional canopy.

The new flat shape is designed to cut drag to a minimum and give the canopy a greater flying speed. As an advanced type of 'chute, it demands careful handling and some experience on the more forgiving P.C. before it is used. In the course of its development, there have been some nasty moments, namely non-openers and malfunctions, since, with all the temperament of a thoroughbred, there have been periods of unreliability with the Cloud-type parachute so it is evidently not a piece of equipment to be toyed with. It is in fact a ram-air parachute and consists of fourteen cells which inflate through mouths at the front of the parachute and taper to smaller apertures at the rear — a sort of double layer canopy, looking rather like a beach li-lo. No doubt it will become as familiar a sight to us as the Para-Commander is now. Its flat large rectangular shape used to give the Cloud rather hard opening characteristics which caused some temporary discomfort depending on the resilience of the jumper. Then those involved in the parachutes' use and design discovered the means to slow the openings and reduce such unpleasant characteristics. The real advantage of the Cloud lies in its greater speed potential — a horizontal speed of 20 to 25 m.p.h. (approximately twice that of the Para-Commander) and rate of descent of 16 to 20 feet per second as compared to the Para-Commander's 13 feet per second. In the case of the Cloud, this figure of 16 to 20 feet per second can be reduced to almost nothing, a fraction before landing, thus eliminating any doubt where stand-up landings are concerned, as well as making for greater accuracy onto the target. By opening and closing mouths and apertures in the canopy, the 'wing' can literally be made to stall on one side and therefore turn or lose height at will. This is where the skill comes in, since quite obviously too much height lost too quickly at the wrong time (i.e. near to the ground or over another parachutist) could prove disastrous. Incidentally, parachutists try never to position themselves directly over or under another parachute since the possibility arises of the lower canopy 'stealing' air and leaving a pocket of low pressure in its wake for the upper canopy to fall into. The upper parachute's rate of descent may then increase sufficiently for it to fall into the lower one and therefore collapse the latter, although the Cloud-type 'chute is something of an exception to this rule. Generally speaking, the more advanced and dynamic ram-air parachutes are likely to be seen more and more as teams like the Falcons introduce them into their displays and master their inherently temperamental tendencies and their unpredictability under certain circumstances. No doubt these sort of characteristics mean months of work and practice before the Cloud can be the vehicle for a large team display — it may yet be proved unsuitable, but either way is unlikely to affect the number of people who flock in their hundreds of thousands each summer to watch these displays. So much for the parachute itself. The means of employing it is of course the ripcord handle, situated close to the capewells on the front of the main harness. Pulling on this allows a number of strong elastics under tension to open the back-pack and this in turn allows the extractor parachutes (themselves under tension through a spring mechanism) to deploy. A similar handle exists for the reserve parachute clipped on to the front of the main harness. The reserve serves as a convenient mounting for the altimeter and stop-watch carried on every descent. On a drop from say 12,000 feet the altimeter needle is referred to from time to time and takes in the region of a minute to slowly unwind from 12,000 feet to 2,000 feet, at which point the needle goes 'into the red' much like a rev. counter in a motor car, and the parachutist knows it is high time to operate the ripcord.

The stop-watch adjacent to the altimeter is used in conjunction with it, confirming the story the altimeter tells and assisting in the timing of manoeuvres such as the bomb-burst.

The red, white and blue smoke trails that accompany each display, stream from three canisters attached to the ankles. A cord attached to the firing mechanism is pulled on exit to fire two of the canisters, enabling those below to follow the descent right from the start. The third canister is fired beneath the open canopy which adds to spectator appeal and demonstrates the manoeuvrability of the canopy as it circles in the sky.

Boots, helmet, gloves and one-piece jumpsuit complete the rig-out. The boots have thick, flat, spongy soles to absorb landing impacts and assist in achieving 'stand ups'. Helmet and goggles are an obvious precaution against collisions with aircraft doors, other parachutists and the ground, the goggles having the additional function of protecting the eyes against powerful slipstreams and free-fall wind rush.

Finally, the jumpsuit itself zips up to ensure that there is no loose clothing to get buffeted about and distract attention or become entangled with equipment. But more than that, it is tailored and shaped to give extra resistance to airflow during free fall which is of particular importance in tracking and

28

relative work. Additionally, the jumpsuit provides admirable protection against grazes, cuts, scrapes and burns when landing heavily on airfield runways!

On the drop zone at each display are items of equipment which play a complementary role. These are the responsibility of the ground party who are in touch with the team leader in the aircraft and are able to communicate the necessary ground conditions information to him. This information includes wind strength and direction both at ground level and jump height.

The ground crew have modern aids at their disposal and work from a Land Rover at the target to calculate the relevant data. There is, for example, a theodolite, able to track a helium-filled balloon and feed accurate information relating to wind conditions.

The same DZ party have the task of preparing the landing area with target crosses and flare, the latter being fired as the aircraft approaches. This assists those in the aircraft in 'spotting' the target, a term which is also used in relation to judging the point of exit as the aircraft flies over the target. Without the flare, the drop zone would frequently be difficult to pick out from 12,000 feet.

The team leader and aircraft navigator, meanwhile, plot information radioed up to them and relate it to aerial photographs of the drop zone.

Final confirmation from the ground that all is ready there and the display can begin. As soon as the team are under canopy, the final piece of equipment comes into use — quite simply a series of canvas sheets with different wind speeds printed on them, visible from the air. The appropriate number is shown to the team depending on ground wind conditions such that they know the sort of landing conditions they will have to face.

There is one other non-essential item of equipment which is used only occasionally — namely the team camera. Some breathtaking and spectacular air-to-air action shots have been achieved by team members appointed to the job, some of whose photographs in this book bear witness to their expertise in this field. Some stunning results have been achieved with both the stills camera (35 mm. motorised Nikon) and the cine (16 mm. Beaulieu). The latter has been responsible for television clips.

Attached to the parachutist's helmet and operated by hand-held press switches, the camera 'sees' and films whatever the parachutist looks at through a special sight mounted on the helmet. If, for example, he wants to film a view of the aircraft as he leaves it, he sets the camera running on exit and looks at the aircraft as he falls away from it, leaving his arms free to take up the normal free-fall position. This would be impossible with a hand-held camera.

So much, then, for the equipment and the manner of its use; what of the men who rely on that equipment for their very survival? Here we delve into that complex subject, personality, and all the facets thereof, and that we must leave for a very separate chapter.

TWO

In the Beginning . . .

In every parachutist's life, there are periods, particularly in our own uncertain climate, when life seems to stand still. Curtains of cloud roll in over the drop zone, winter winds mount their annual assault and the daily meteorological checks each tell the same frustrating story — no jumping.

Such was the case one dismal February morning on my arrival at Brize Norton in Oxfordshire. A sprawling and, like most R.A.F. camps, strangely nostalgic and compelling place, Brize Norton on this particular morning seemed even more austere than usual. The welcome, however, was warm, despite the fact that I had, I later realised, parked my car in the Officer Commanding's slot. Yes, I was informed by Simon Bales, team leader, a youthful and fresh-faced flight-lieutenant, February did tend to be a quiet period jump-wise. Some of the team were away on leave, the display season would not be under way for some weeks and training jumps were frequently aborted because of foul weather. Consequently, this was a time for preparation and administration, but things would no doubt be livening up soon. I looked forward to that with some relish. By the look of some of the photographs on the walls of the Falcons' headquarters, when things did start happening, they would be rather special. For although Simon's office and indeed all of the Falcons' administration block was an ordinary enough place with nothing to suggest one of the world's foremost parachute teams, the photographs on the walls told a different story. They showed in colourful and graphic detail all the skill, grace and charismatic appeal that pulls in the crowds between April and October every year; men apparently dangling in mid-air, faces contorted by the 120 m.p.h. rush of air, yet smiling happily behind their goggles; others teetering on the edge of space prior to exit, seemingly unconcerned although, I suspect, nursing varying degrees of apprehension. One souvenir in particular is especially appealing — a shield from that parachutist's paradise, the Southern Californian desert where the Falcons go on detachment for concentrated training. Inscribed on this shield are the wistful words, "It never rains in Southern California."

For the present, however, we had to accept what our less temperate climes had to offer, which meant a visit to the place where there is usually a lot of action going on regardless of the weather, the main hangar where the Falcons and their fellow parachute-jumping instructors are involved with the training of airborne troops.

The place was alive with activity with squads of men undergoing all the pre-jump practices that trainees must master. Despite or because of the intense level of activity, there was little evidence of the excessive and unnecessary military discipline so evident in some military establishments. On the contrary, the relationship between the trainee and the instructor is surprisingly relaxed and testimony to the control and man-management of the instructors. Perhaps the daunting and, to some, awesome prospect of leaping from a perfectly serviceable aircraft has its own disciplining effect on the troops and they do not therefore feel inclined to horse-play. I was amused to find, though, that the humorous dialogue between instructor and pupil had not changed since my own Forces days ten years before.

Broadly-grinning instructor to pupil after sweaty session in a mock Hercules fuselage: "Enjoy that, McIntyre?"

McIntyre, sweating copiously beneath overlarge helmet and only just visible behind equipment container almost as large as himself: "Did Ah buggery!"

Instructor's grin grows even broader, McIntyre studies floor sheepishly, twenty other would-be paratroopers grin in unison.

Dominating the proceedings in the hangar is the same Hercules training fuselage, identical to the genuine thing, from whence there emerges at intervals a port and starboard 'stick' of twenty-five or so parachutists, heavily laden with equipment, rifle, and dummy parachutes front and rear. Apart from height above ground, everything in the fuselage is an accurate simulation of the real thing and once inside, airborne troops can practise drills such as hooking up the static line which opens the parachute automatically, or securing the equipment they must take into battle and which is released on exit to dangle below them on a rope.

Surrounding the 'Hercules' is a variety of training equipment; ramps and steps for landing practices, suspended harnesses for swinging in and rings for swinging on, but most significant of all the slightly formidable-looking 'fan' exit trainer high up in the roof of the hangar. It consists of a mock aircraft doorway where the soldier is given some idea of what it feels like to make that all-important step into the void. Although the apparatus is not intimidating, and landings from it rather gentle, refusals are not unknown, in which case the pupil is deemed not suitable for parachuting and is returned to the unit whence he came. Generally, however, it is considered rather fun, although I saw few faces that did not register some apprehension. The 30-foot fan is so called because the soldier's descent is slowed by a rapidly revolving blade which catches air as it rotates and hinders the paying-out of the wire attached to the pupil's harness.

Finally, and perhaps most ominous of the indoor equipment, the innocent-looking but dreaded balloon cage lurked menacingly at the end of the hangar. A more subtle instrument of torture, it is said, has yet to be devised. It does have the property, however, of quickly curing those airborne troops afflicted by constipation. It is quite simply a cage just large enough to hold four troops on their first descents, who are hoisted in terrifying silence to 800 feet by a barrage balloon, to make their exits via a door at the front of the cage or a hole in the floor.

More of that anon however for there is one more exit simulator, this time outside, where trainees are hurled violently along a wire stretching from the top of a 40-foot tower to a point near the ground some seventy yards away. Leaping from the tower with harness attached to the wire via a pulley wheel, the pupil holds a tight, compact position regardless of how he is thrown about as he travels along the wire and in this way hopes to simulate the buffeting of the slipstream. When it comes to the actual jump he is thus likely to be spun, inverted or generally disorientated but can get on with the job of descending safely and preparing for his ground battle role. Incidentally, the slipstream trainer is known inevitably as the knacker-cracker and is one of two pieces of outdoor equipment. The other is the under-the-canopy flight trainer consisting of a 70-foot tower from the top of which the pupil steps off to swing in a harness as though suspended in a parachute. He can then practise his all-round observation drills and canopy-checking routine until he is allowed to descend at about the same rate as a real parachute to practise both canopy-handling and the technique of the all-important landing roll.

For the most part however the troops and their instructors are in the hangar where I now sat taking in the atmosphere of new paint and rubber landing mats. It was strangely silent now after the day-long turmoil of troops in heavy boots thumping about the place. Some were now ready for their first descents, initially from the balloon at Weston-on-the-Green in Oxfordshire, then from an aircraft at the same drop zone. I would be airborne to watch that at the first opportunity and the blood began to run a little quicker even now at the thought of it. That day was not far away.

THREE

'H.A.L.O.' Interlude

After weeks of teeming rain and dark skies, the last morning in February finally delivered the goods. The day dawned clear, calm and sunny — bang on schedule for training jumps from 12,000 feet onto Salisbury Plain. The Falcons were to put in two drops using the season's projected display pattern of a bomb-burst with a central core of six relative workers linking up.

Additionally, the remainder of the instructors not actually in the display team were to do two 'H.A.L.O.' (High Altitude, Low Opening) drops from 25,000 feet, complete with oxygen.

The atmosphere at headquarters was alive as jumpsuits were donned and parachutes fitted. Most of the jumpers were experienced, some appearing blasé about the whole thing. Others were going from 25,000 with only a handful of jumps behind them.

By 9.30, everyone was ready to emplane whilst I accompanied the ground party and ambulance to Fox Covert, a remote training area on Salisbury Plain. P-hour, the time scheduled for the first jump, was eleven o'clock, but as the hour came and went it became evident that there were problems. The Land Rover radio that had accompanied us to the drop zone had gone US (unserviceable). I remembered the earlier warning of drop-zone N.C.O. Martin Daccus, known to all as 'Sid' — "In this job there are always buggeration factors". I wasn't altogether familiar with the term but had to admit it fairly described the current predicament, for by now the aircraft should be overhead waiting for the all-clear from the ground but we were as yet unable to make contact. Sid set about the stand-by radio feverishly only to find it completely unresponsive. He swore quietly, cursing equipment that proved temperamental when he needed it most.

Meanwhile, DZ officer for the day, Flight-Lieutenant John Parry, had been tinkering with the main radio. For some inexplicable reason it suddenly buzzed into life. Panic over! We need not have worried. The aircraft had not yet taken off because of engine trouble, but a new P-hour had been set for midday. Sighs of relief all round.

It had not escaped our notice, however, that winds had been building up steadily over the last hour. The anemometer showed 17 knots (right on the limit) with gusts of 23 knots. A tricky decision for the DZ officer whose responsibility it was to ensure that the jump did not take place if winds were too high. A final check showed a steady 18 knots.

"That settles it — I'll tell 'em not to take off!" Flight-Lieutenant Parry contacted Salisbury Ops. Too late. The aircraft was on its way having taken off fifteen minutes earlier. We scanned the skies and strained with our ears until moments later we could hear the steady drone of the Hercules's approach, its cargo of thirty parachutists keyed up and ready to go. The thought of cancelling everything at this stage appalled. Another wind check showed very slight moderation, 14 to 16 knots — just jumpable for the Falcons, but the high-altitude men would be disappointed. Some of them were on less advanced canopies than the Para-Commander and were less experienced. For them there would be the frustration of returning to base with the aircraft to let all the accumulated adrenalin subside.

For the Falcons, however, there was no going back. From Flight-Lieutenant Parry on the radio came the magic words, "This is Fox Covert. Windspeed has moderated to 14 to 16 knots. You are clear to jump." Sid dashed across from the Land Rover to the targets and ignited two smoke flares. The aircraft appeared overhead almost immediately, at 12,000 feet still quite a large object in the sky. I could not help thinking she was a little too far over to the left until I noticed a series of twitches which were bringing the Hercules's nose round slightly to line her up more on the target. At this point, Simon Bales would be kneeling at the port door giving instructions to the pilot (five degrees left, five degrees right or whatever, as necessary) his heart no doubt banging away furiously and the adrenalin flooding his bloodstream. Meanwhile, Davie Ross, heavily moustachioed Flight-Sergeant of the team and one of its most experienced jumpers, would be at the starboard door giving a second opinion if needed.

Suddenly, incredibly, they were out! A dozen tiny dots hurtling earthward, almost invisible in fact, since display 'smokes' were not being used. Sid let out a groan, "Too far over. They'll never get in."

As canopies began to mushroom 2,500 feet above us, I began to realise what he meant. They were all trying to sideslip and crab awkwardly across the sky, clawing every last bit of drive from their P.C.s. All to no avail, however, the wind just would not let them make significant headway and it was clear most would land well wide of target. At 1,000 feet there seemed to be parachutes all over Salisbury Plain. One disappeared behind a copse over a mile away, most of the rest were scattered about in all directions and were being blown even further away. I had a sneaking suspicion that the wind was becoming stronger by the minute. Directly over me at about 500 feet, Sergeant Alistair MacDonald gazed down at the rapidly receding target. He was facing directly into the wind to keep his speed to a minimum, but even so was travelling backwards alarmingly quickly. Not a man to be intimidated by such a minor detail, Alistair waved unconcernedly. "B y e e e e . . ." he shouted at us as he disappeared over the other side of a hill. He reappeared with all the others some fifteen to twenty minutes later. Some were cursing good-naturedly. One or two were a bit disgruntled. All were O.K. though, despite some fearsome landings. Only Tommy Johnston had 'got in'. Remarkably, he was within a few yards of the target. He had turned into wind only a few feet above the ground and his canopy 'brakes' were not fully operational as he landed. The resultant impact left me in considerable doubt as to his welfare, but Tommy, a tough, determined, Scot, stood up and started to bundle up his 'chute ready for the next jump.

Making our way back to the bus waiting to take the team to Boscombe Down to re-emplane, the consensus was that the aircraft had been nearly a mile from where it should have been when the team had stepped out. One or two of the team had realised this straightaway and spent the greater part of the free fall tracking towards a good opening point, effectively 'throwing the display away' but at least giving themselves a good chance of making the target. The rest, for the most part, had followed the display routine.

It transpired that Simon Bales's throat microphone had failed and the pilot did not therefore get the vital directions on the run-in. No matter. Get keyed up for the next one and try again!

Back at Boscombe Down where the Hercules had landed, the high-altitude men who had not jumped sat somewhat dejectedly with their packed lunches. Some were 'dripping' (moaning) as is generally the wont of military personnel. I could understand their disappointment after getting completely kitted up with parachutes, oxygen and all, and particularly after watching the Falcons go out. H.A.L.O. jumper Sergeant Kirk was letting rip at an officer. But then, as one parachute-jumping instructor put it to me, he usually was. A bit of a character, John Kirk. I had first met him twelve years before when he had put me through my paces at Abingdon. I was glad to see he had not changed. "Bloody civvies," he remarked when I saw him in the Mess, "I told you to get your 'air cut twelve years ago and you *still* 'aven't." In contrast, affable Flight-Lieutenant Vic Last seemed remarkably unconcerned about the whole affair, despite the fact that it was to have been his first 25,000-footer that morning.

"I don't think about a jump until it's about to take place, so

I don't have time to worry about it."

Didn't he *ever* get worried?

"In the balloon because it's so cold-blooded. No noise or movement to divert your attention. Nearly everyone gets nervous in the balloon."

It was time to get back on the road for the afternoon's proceedings.

D Z Officer John Parry addressed the high-altitude men.

"We'll try and get you out this afternoon but if the winds are over the limit I'm afraid I will definitely not be giving the All Clear."

Half an hour later the ground party was back at Fox Covert where to our dismay the winds were, if anything, slightly greater than in the morning. At P-hour, 3 p.m. the hoped-for lull in wind-speed came almost miraculously, and as the Hercules appeared overhead the anemometer was recording 12 to 14 knots. Everything was Go!

The Falcons duly appeared in the sky on schedule. Immediately, it was pretty clear that they were again well off to one side of the wind-line; not quite as much as in the earlier drop, but they were going to have to fight their way across the wind to line up on target. This time they were ready to do just that, however, and the outward trackers moving away from target turned earlier to track back in. One by one, canopies appeared in the sky. Again the sideways crabbing to line up on target — this time it looked as though they were all going to make it. Some of the landings were going to be a little 'hairy' — the accursed wind was up to its tricks again — but as far as the target was concerned, they would all be there or thereabouts.

John Gregor was first in, right on the button! A sergeant in his early thirties, John would deputise in the absence of the official free-fall photographer. Now he swung over the smoke flares, only fifty or sixty feet above us. He peered down intently at the rapidly-approaching ground.

"Away, Sid." He shouted a warning in case Sid hadn't seen

39

him, and moments later he was down cleanly, impressively, painlessly. Some of the others were not so fortunate. Davie Ross came in hard, right behind John Gregor. He was travelling backwards fast and I watched his landing with interest. He appeared to go in swift succession from feet to rump to helmet at which point he was for an instant in a curiously inverted vertical position. As he observed at de-brief in the bus afterwards, "That's the first time I've done a stand-up landing on my head." He had grinned cheerfully, displaying remarkable physical resilience for a man in his early forties.

Following Davie's landing, the target suddenly seemed saturated with canopies and for some seconds all hell was let loose as bodies piled in around us and as a succession of thumps signalled each landing. Someone's canopy failed to deflate on landing and it began to disappear over the crest of a nearby dip, dragging its human cargo with it.

"He'll have to capewell," observed John Parry, and as he spoke the canopy appeared to accelerate and leave its load behind, to collapse in a limp heap of nylon some seconds later.

Within ten minutes, everyone was gathered at the Land Rover, breathing heavily but discussing the jump enthusiastically. It had been pretty heady stuff to watch and the team were exhilarated. They had waited a long time for a day like today and it felt good to be back in action. John Gregor wanted to know if the winds were too far over the limit for training with the team 'Frisbee', a comment which was a source of some amusement.

The chatter continued as we made our way across to the bus, half a mile away, for de-brief.

"Flight-Sergeant and cripples first," quipped Davie Ross as everyone clambered aboard.

"Flight-Sergeants *are* cripples," returned team leader Bales immediately. I couldn't help thinking that even if they weren't, they soon would be if they made many more landings like Flight-Sergeant Ross had just made. Even so, in those sort of winds, any landing you got up and walked away from was a good one.

Meanwhile, 25,000 feet above us, the H.A.L.O. men had
the All Clear to drop. The Hercules was still easily visible even
at that height. The parachutists, we knew, would hardly be
visible at all. I made the mistake of taking my eye off the aircraft for a few seconds just as they exited and once that happens there is little chance of picking them up in the sky.

Those who saw the tiny, tiny dots on exit followed that incredibly long free fall of two full minutes. Most of us had to
wait a further minute or so until they were down to 12,000 or
10,000 feet. The H.A.L.O. parachutist is a totally different
concept to the display parachutist in that he is not meant to be
seen from the ground. The Special Air Service particularly,
have men trained in H.A.L.O. work, their rôle being to land
in enemy territory secretly. On this particular day, they may
have landed secretly, but they would have had quite a trek to
reach their destination. When their parachutes opened they
were, literally, miles away, with no hope whatsoever of getting
in. Either they had undergone a lot of free-fall drift or the
target flares for the correct landing point had proved invisible
from five miles up. Bunched fairly close together, they descended slowly behind a wood some two or three miles away.
Under their large, 30-foot canopies with slower rate of descent
and less manoeuvrability than the Para-Commanders, they had
not been able to make up any of the distance between us and
them. We watched two more H.A.L.O. men landing on the
side of a hill about a mile away, separated from the main
group. One turned into wind to land.

"Christ!" someone said as the second of the two prepared to
land. "He's driving with the wind."

We all winced in sympathy as number two hit Salisbury
Plain at a speed greater than is normally considered healthy.
He had forgotten to turn his canopy into the wind. To the surprise of nearly everybody, he was up immediately and rolling
up his 'chute. Twenty minutes later he climbed aboard the bus
to howls of good-natured derision.

41

With all of the Falcons at least back on the bus, it was time for a quick run-down of the drop, discussing things that went wrong or could be improved next time. It was generally agreed that they had all had to fight their way in since they had for the most part found themselves on the wrong side of the opening point. Simon was happy with the drop, being, as it was, only the second U.K. drop since Christmas, and in very trying conditions at that. One or two of the team were not entirely happy at some of the free-fall team-positioning and said so in no uncertain terms.

All good man to man stuff with nobody pulling rank or mincing words and nobody taking umbrage at plain speaking. A team like the Falcons cannot afford undercurrents of unrest and here, at the end of the day de-brief, their commitment to togetherness and teamwork showed. When the display season came along, that sort of co-operation would make the difference between a successful display with everyone on target and a not so successful display with half of the team not getting in. When it came to places like the Colchester Military Tattoo with its very small arena, failing to make the target would mean at best an embarrassing landing out of the arena and at worst a potentially dangerous situation. Now was the time to reduce the risk of that happening to an absolute minimum. It would mean a lot of hard work and constant practice but, come the day, they would be ready, of that, I was certain.

FOUR

"... just big, useless lumps."

One of the most important factors governing a man's contentment or disenchantment with his lot is his love for the work that he does. If this is absent, life is empty indeed. In this respect the Falcons are of the select few who truly do for a living something that they would do for pleasure anyway. In fact a number of the team do parachute with civilian or Forces' clubs in their spare time and that sort of involvement in and commitment to their work tends to make itself felt in their individual personalities. They seem, to a man, a happy and dedicated crew despite occasional protestations to the contrary — when they are parachuting that is. When, through circumstances outside their control they are not parachuting, the frustration shows. It is almost as if all the nervous energy that they carry around with them each day in preparation for their jumps has to be diverted elsewhere for release.

Such was the case for most of March, a month of cold and drizzle and wind and consequently a frustratingly immobile month for the Falcons. Time was getting short for the final piecing together of display rehearsals in preparation for the season only five weeks or so away. The new members of the team were short on practice, the more experienced men impatient to be jumping again. In the meantime they all had to keep in top condition physically which meant regular workouts at the station gymnasium, afternoons of volleyball or five-a-side soccer and the like; games of which none were meant to be taken seriously but which nevertheless soon developed into stern physical confrontations as competitive and basically aggressive natures began to make their presence felt. Consciousness of rank went out of the window as bodies were sent

43

sprawling inelegantly on the stone floor. Under such circumstances the Falcons immediately impress as individuals who are completely at home in the physically-orientated confines of a gymnasium which is hardly surprising considering their backgrounds as physical education specialists. What is surprising, however, is the wide variation of physical types within the team. Although all are basically mesomorphic (that is with a tendency to muscularity of physique) thay range from the slight but wiry Joe McCready (one of the relative men) to the tall, angular and powerful frame of Sid who displays remarkable agility for a man of his size. Between the two extremes, the team runs through the whole spectrum of physical shapes, sizes and abilities, but generally with a bias toward stockiness like John Conrad (team manager and drop zone officer); Graham Pierce (gymnast, relative worker and stills photographer); Bob Kent ('Bionic Bob', relative worker built like a tank and with a tendency to drop like a brick!); Trevor Green (survival equipment fitter with the DZ party); John Gregor (relative worker, former R.A.F. judo representative and rugby player); and Simon Bales (team leader and all-round sportsman).

Of the remainder, all sportsmen and athletes in their own right, Phil Kelly, Tommy Johnston, Alistair MacDonald and Steve Rowe tend to be taller but less aggressively muscular. Deputy team leader Roger Nicolle, senior team N.C.O. Dave Ross and Dave Armstrong (all trackers on display jumps) seem to achieve a happy balance physically without particular, out of the ordinary characteristics—that is until they get to work at what they know best; then it is a different story, with all the ingrained skill and expertise pushing itself irresistibly to the fore whether they be careering across the sky at 70 m.p.h. or completing subtle, minor adjustments to control toggles to facilitate the most graceful (usually) of landings.

The message is that, from a purely physical point of view, the Falcons do not need to be of any particular type to achieve their expertise. On the contrary, what does set them apart from the man in the street is their mental capabilities enabling them to harden their minds to the stresses and potential dangers involved in parachuting until the act of jumping from an aircraft is a natural part of their lives.

Surprisingly, not all of the team are as vastly experienced as might be supposed. Dave Ross, Bob Kent, Joe McCready and Graham Pierce have all completed a thousand or more descents, but for many of the team, two to four hundred drops is the norm which in parachuting circles is only average. All the more noteworthy, then, the reputation they have built for themselves as one of the world's leading display teams.

Talking of vastness of experience, mention must be made at this point of the remarkable performance of safety worker Trevor Green on his first descent. Although not a display jumper, his duties largely being concerned with ground back-up, he was one of the first to learn to parachute through a revolutionary and remarkably rapid training schedule. This entails the usual pre-jump ground drills, free-fall positioning, landing practices and the like, a matter of a very few days of concentrated instruction. This is followed, as was the case with Trevor Green, by the first jump; not just a static-line jump or a five-second delay; not even a thirty-second delay. In Trevor's case, the first jump meant a full one-minute delay from 12,000 feet. During that minute he was able to remain stable throughout. If things had gone wrong (for example if he had lost consciousness through violent spinning) an automatic opening device would have opened his parachute with the change in barometric pressure at about 2,000 feet. This method of training is in the offing as the accepted way of introducing free fall to Forces personnel.

To get some idea of the revolutionary nature of this method a look at the current training schedule for civilian parachutists shows a lengthy and somewhat inflexible system of progressions for even the most able learners. For example, a novice who displays perfect progress must complete at present a minimum of six static-line descents before moving on to three-second delays, five-second delays and so on in gradual steps, possibly a necessarily expensive and time-consuming operation but something of a chore for the individual capable of Trevor Green's feat.

On the subject of first jumps it is interesting to note individual reactions to the feelings of trepidation which are inevitable. Most of the team admit to experiencing an intense feeling of apprehension not far removed from real fear immediately prior to their first few descents. The classic symptoms of dry mouth, vague feelings of nausea, the desire to sleep or yawn in the aircraft, loosening of the bowels and the accompanying gut reaction in the pit of the stomach — some or all of these adrenalin-induced feelings of anxiety make their presence felt in every parachutist at some time and the Falcons are no exception. Generally, however, the fear of those initial jumps steadily develops into something more akin to pleasurable excitement. True, the varying degrees of tension and nervousness are seldom far away but this is in itself a blessing since such feelings are a constant reminder of the potential dangers involved and they effectively discourage over-confidence.

Tests on both experienced and novice parachutists have indicated a heartbeat close to two hundred per minute as exit becomes imminent, a rate approaching that of an exhausted athlete after a prolonged bout of sprinting at maximum speed. Perhaps this is an indication of how hard the body works to prepare itself for what is to come but the strange thing is that as soon as the parachutist has settled down into free fall his pulse rate drops considerably until the time comes to pull, at which point it generally rises again. It is as if the actual stepping from the aircraft is the high point (pun not intentional) of parachuting. That crisis over the actual fall is by contrast almost an exercise in relaxation, particularly for the seasoned jumper. For the Falcons, this relaxation phase is taken up largely by the various specific tasks allotted to them; tasks such as manoeuvring for the link-up in the case of the relative workers and tracking across the sky to the right opening point in the case of the Bomb-Burst men.

Personality-wise, parachutists tend to be of a type and the Falcons generally are true to the rule. Almost without exception they are extrovert by nature to varying degrees. They laugh easily and there are some pretty hilarious nights out after displays. Organisers of shows at which the Falcons appear frequently lay on free beer, one perk of the job which is greatly appreciated, the more so since the team do not receive extra money for their parachuting duties. They do receive a lot of public acclaim, particularly in the summer months when they are constantly in the public eye. Like all entertainers the team love to perform to an audience, so the glamour and publicity of the display season is a great morale-booster. Places such as Biggin Hill attract crowds larger than that of a Wembley cup final; the Paris Air Show where the team appear each year boasts hundreds of thousands of spectators. Taking into account these and fifty or more other display appearances over the year, the total number of people the team perform to each year runs into millions. There is seldom, however, any sign of all the fuss going to their heads and causing inflated egos. Naturally, they love the acclaim that sometimes surrounds them at displays but any flashy or big-headed talk would immediately be recognised as such by their colleagues and become a target for derision.

The Falcons as a team generally tend to have the rise taken out of them by various of their colleagues for being the glamour boys of the R.A.F. whilst others get on with the more mundane work. Criticism levelled at the team is often tongue in cheek, sometimes born of envy and occasionally the result of genuine grievance. If there is a problem over availability of a single aircraft with a number of parties requiring its services, the Falcons frequently have priority, particularly when short of display practice. A good week of continual jumping, however, is just as likely to put them at the bottom of the pile whilst other parachutists take priority. Either way, privileged or no, the competition for getting on to the team is fairly high since it affords a marvellous opportunity for those wishing to be purely professional parachutists for at least two years.

There are few laid-down qualifications to be met before joining the team apart from being a potentially proficient display parachutist. Equally important is the ability to integrate within a team and to be a tolerably relaxed and easy-going person to work with. Additionally and significantly all of the team have a background of success in one or more spheres, be it sporting or academic, prior to joining the Falcons. They are used to being 'good' at something whether it be squash, rugby, gymnastics or some related activity, which is possibly an aid to keeping their feet firmly on the ground rather than being carried away by their own sudden rise to 'fame' on joining the team.

In the final analysis, however, all can never be sweetness and light and the Falcons have their share of upsets and disagreements. When there are differences of opinion they are aired uncompromisingly and verbal set-tos are not infrequent. Post-jump de-briefs particularly become heated as ideas are thrashed out with (usually) a refreshing absence of pompous standing on rank. The occasional acid remark and outright insult was usually in the air at briefings and when it was, the ebullient and abrasive but equally likeable John Gregor was usually in there somewhere.

One bone of contention particularly in the relative group (the link-up men forming the central core of the bomb-burst) was the occasional failure to achieve a full six-man link in practices. The main problem, it seemed, was the tendency of the first two men to link (the base and pin), to turn slowly as they were in free fall. This made further linking up difficult for the remaining four who were having to turn with the base and pin in order to get in. The problem was, should the remaining four try and stay with the turn to link with the partner decided upon beforehand, or should they go straight for the link regardless of how the base and pin turned. In the latter case they could find themselves linking on the wrong side of the base and pin. Graham Pierce was for disregarding the turn and going straight in whilst John Gregor favoured turning with the base to enable docking on the same side of it each time.

"For Christ's sake," urged John, "why the hell not follow the turn; we're all experienced parachutists and it shouldn't cause too many problems."

"Because," returned Graham, "we could end up chasing each other around the bloody sky, that's why."

The feathers flew for a while. John swore in exasperation and got up to leave but realising the futility of that sat down again. Joe McCready, level-headed and tactful, tried to put the discussion on a less heated footing. Graham, ever professional in matters parachuting, maintained his stance. Why waste time getting the six relative men together? To follow the turn could add seconds on to the time needed for link-up. The problem was thrashed out eventually to a mutually acceptable solution; the base and pin would have to minimise any turning tendencies as soon as possible whilst those coming in to dock would let the base and pin settle down before attempting to complete the link.

Solving minor problems such as this is an accepted part of the Falcons' lives and although differences of opinion frequently occur, they remain secondary to the unity of the team. A typical example is when caps are off and the whole team are together in the gymnasium. The insults often fly quite liberally, usually good-natured but sometimes less so, particularly in non-jumping periods when they tend to work out their frustrations on each other. No-one appears to take offence however, it is all so much water off a duck's back. It was often amusing to watch the team in the gymnasium hurtling into each other, occasionally cursing or hurling insults. Sometimes it was difficult to tell if these were in earnest or tongue in cheek but no-one seemed to care either way. In these sort of circumstances officers neither expected nor gave any quarter. Physically as robust as any in the team, they were well able to take care of themselves. On the other hand, they did occasionally come in for some unmerciful mickey-taking as a result of the 'howlers' that commissioned officers in the Forces seem to let slip unintentionally. One recent 'gem' was the unfortunate concluding remark of an anonymous officer who rounded off a briefing with the immortal words: "The decision is maybe and that's final!" That one would certainly take some living down.

The team as a whole take the mickey out of each other constantly but no-one takes it to heart. Davie Ross's extravagant moustache, naturally enough, is a prime target. Rumour had it that he grew it to hide a nervous twitch caused by years of jumping, an accusation which just made the offended party's grin grow a little broader. Similarly, Dave Armstrong's receding hairline was said to be the result of traumatic jumping experiences, the truth of which one tended to doubt since he is a singularly relaxed and composed individual. Like the rest of the team, he is surprisingly unself-conscious about the prowess of the Falcons. As Alistair MacDonald put it: "There are a couple of gymnasts on the team, the rest of us are just big useless lumps." Far from the truth of course but an indication of their easy-going approach to life.

FIVE

A Day in the Life of

Predictably, March came in like a lion. Consulting the meteorological experts was frequently just a formality. One had only to watch the clouds racing by overhead to know that there would be little chance of any drops taking place on a particular day. Almost all of the first week was a dead one as far as parachuting was concerned, until on the second Monday the prospect began to appear a little brighter. At least the team managed to get up in the air and were over the Weston-on-the-Green dropping zone before a combination of cloud and wind brought them home again. They would try again later; with any luck I would be on that second, hopefully more fruitful lift. For the moment, however, it would be necessary to have myself included on the flight manifest with the Falcons. The loadmaster in the Hercules would need to know who and what was going up in the aircraft in terms of weight and numbers, since this would naturally affect the aircraft's trim.

Across at the Ops room, Sergeant Mike McClean added my name to the manifest sheet. In the adjacent hangar, the Falcons were kitting up for the second time and moments later were making their way across the tarmac to the waiting Hercules. We climbed aboard via the huge, gaping tailgate. The team was relaxed and the light-hearted banter belied the formidable task just fifteen minutes away. Soon, however, all casual talk had to stop as engines started up and the whine of the turbine rose to a high-pitched crescendo, drowning all normal conversation. It was a case of shout or not be heard and the Falcons were content now to sit quietly with their own thoughts as the usual, exhilarating, pre-jump atmosphere made itself felt. Only Simon Bales continued to talk by means of the throat microphone with which he would be in touch with the pilot at all times.

The tailgate closed ominously and the Hercules taxied to the runway for take-off. The noise and acceleration of a Hercules on take-off is impressive and rather awe-inspiring, yet still every face remained impassive and unmoved. I could not help wondering if those bland, blasé exteriors were hiding, to a degree, at least some of the trauma that I was feeling — and I was just a spectator.

The aircraft quickly levelled out. Most of the team were on their feet making the usual pre-jump checks of themselves and each other. Tommy Johnston was checker for the day and therefore not yet kitted-up. Instead, he would go to each team member and ensure that his equipment was absolutely fault-free.

This accomplished, the team sat peacefully to await arrival over the target. That moment seemed to be taking a long time to arrive and the reason soon became clear. At 12,000 feet there was thick cloud cover. We would have to go down to 10,000 feet. That in itself was something of a problem since Weston-on-the-Green is uncomfortably close to one of the world's busiest airports, that of Kidlington in Oxfordshire, where thousands of light aeroplanes take off and land each year. The pilot was having to wait for clearance from ground control in order to descend at a time when so many other aircraft were in the vicinity. In the meantime, we would have to content ourselves with circling at 12,000 feet.

It was interesting to note the different reactions that this brought from the team. Some, perhaps impatient at being confined in the aircraft already for the best part of an hour, stood up to gaze out of the windows at the white opaqueness of the clouds, probably hoping to catch a glimpse of the target in a convenient gap in the clouds. Others sought solace in sleep. Bob Kent (base man and first out of the aircraft) had dozed peacefully since take-off and continued to do so now. On the seat next to me, team leader Simon Bales had finished his ten-minute nap and was now busily recording wind speeds and directions at different heights over the target. This information went on to his aerial photograph of Weston DZ and would be made available for all to see prior to jumping. For the moment, Simon was the one with the pressing responsibility of processing all the information coming up from the ground party to him via the pilot. For the most part, the remainder of the team sat thoughtfully now, composed and meditative in curious contrast to the frantic roar of the engines. A heavy atmosphere of controlled nerves was irresistible. A single yawn in the aircraft started off a chain reaction and I experienced a strange, inexplicable desire to sleep, probably the same nervous reaction I had noticed before in parachutists.

From time to time, individuals would walk over to the tubes to take in oxygen, since at 12,000 feet the lack of air was inclined to make itself felt. As it happened, we were at the maximum height permitted without the use of oxygen masks and the rarity of the atmosphere was now noticeable, as was the fairly sharp drop in temperature. It was the sort of 'on-off' situation with which I was beginning to become familiar, another of the buggeration factors that went with the job. It was a time for few words. Even the normally hyper-active Davie Ross dozed briefly. The youthful-looking Phil Kelly, a tall, fair sergeant, made his way along the fuselage. "Thick cloud cover," he gestured pessimistically, and walked across to the small latrine set into the side of the fuselage to relieve himself nonchalantly. I was reminded that I was in dire need myself and was about to repeat the operation when it began to look as though things might be happening. Simon was on his feet indicating to the rest of the team that we were to descend to 10,000 feet or as low as was necessary to get under the cloud cover. This was down to 1,500 feet in places but there were apparently gaps over the drop zone. Simon wrote on his DZ photo: "We are spiralling down looking for gaps in the cloud".

The message was passed round. I was amused to see that Bob Kent was still sleeping blissfully. Known as the team 'heavy' and ribbed unmercifully as 'The Bionic Man' Bob it was who organised DZ photos such as the one being passed round now. Under the canopy, he had a distinct tendency to descend somewhat faster than his colleagues, a source of some amusement to them.

Suddenly, the message came through. The jump was on and the target was visible from 10,000 feet. Better than we had hoped. The whole team were on their feet, ready and waiting to go. Despatcher and loadmaster Mike McClean went over to port and starboard doors to lift them clear of the fuselage. Immediately, the roar of the slipstream rose to drown everything else, tearing relentlessly at anything or anyone approaching the door.

As one, the whole team moved to gather by the doors, peering at the earth two miles below for a glimpse of the target, or pouring over the DZ photo to get a mental picture of opening points.

From my seat directly adjacent to the port door, I had the most incredible view of both the target and the men who were soon to be hurtling towards that target at speeds of 150 m.p.h. and more. Sid had evidently been getting to work with the flares and the horizontal smoke was a clear indication of fairly strong winds. Close by, it was just possible to pick out the barrage balloons used at Weston for taking the four-man cage up for static-line jumpers.

Simon Bales and Davie Ross were kneeling in the doors now, heads in their respective slipstreams 'eye balling' the target. The red light came on, indicating that flight direction was now in Simon's hands. He would take the Hercules over the target on a dummy run, whilst the ten standing team members grouped on the tailgate, five facing the port door and five facing the starboard door. No time for joking or dozing now. The tension and concentration on those ten faces was overwhelming. Now was the point of no return. The blood was up, adrenalin was pouring into the system and pulse rates hammering away frantically.

The dummy run completed satisfactorily, the Hercules dipped a wing to complete a circuit and lined up on target for the run-in proper. Bob Kent stood at the port door, bracing himself. As base man, he would be first out whilst his opposite number, John Gregor, at the starboard door would exit fractionally after Bob to start the four-man or six-man central link in the bomb-burst. Bob was one of the bespectacled members of the team and he gazed down through his spectacles now at the rolling, green expanse of Weston. Suddenly the green light was on — the Hercules was over the target. Simon would give it another few seconds to allow for the strong wind-drift the team would undergo under their canopies. A couple of quick, final, directional adjustments to the pilot and Simon, and David Ross were on their feet, unplugging their microphones and casting them to one side. This was it. The waiting was over. Everyone was almost bursting to get out. The smoke carriers stood with fingers 'on the triggers' of their canisters. All eyes were on the team leader and fifteen seconds late of the green light, he gave the thumbs up. A number of distinct pops could be heard as smokes were triggered off, and suddenly everything seemed to happen at once. I sat pop-eyed and exhilarated with mind boggling as one by one in rapid succession the Falcons hurled themselves clear of the aircraft to be torn away by the slipstream. For a few brief seconds they were under threat of being tossed about like leaves in the wind, but basic stability and direction remained constant regardless of this.

From my Hercules eye-view, I had the privilege of seeing the whole thing from above. There was no question of settling into a straight forward fall at any time during the forty-five second delay. They were obviously working for position the instant they were out of the aircraft. I was strongly aware of Bob Kent only a few feet outside the aircraft amidst all the turbulence of the slipstream, his head turning to the left as he looked for

John Gregor. He might have been asleep in the aircraft but he was certainly switched-on out of the aircraft. There suddenly seemed to be bodies everywhere falling away from the aircraft and growing smaller by the second. Simon Bales was last man out. At the door, he turned and nodded nonchalantly, triggered his smoke canister and was gone. I really do believe he was grinning up at me from the slipstream as I watched from the door until he turned away for the bomb-burst, his outward track traced by the usual blue smoke.

I gazed somewhat in awe at the rapidly receding figures far below and wondered at the things a man is capable of if he is single-minded enough. It is indeed an impressive sight to watch a human being functioning at full physical and mental efficiency more than two miles above the ground with a 120 m.p.h. 'wind' trying to disorientate and unbalance him and with no other means of self-preservation than a small pack of nylon on his back. There can be few greater physical challenges. Certainly, the proceedings which I was watching from my vantage point in the belly of the aircraft, provided the single most impressive visual impact I have ever experienced.

The next time the reader is at the top of a very tall building it may be an interesting exercise to look down at the ground and imagine stepping into the void below. The natural human instinct faced with such a falling situation, is to react by closing the eyes, switching off all coherent thought and taking up a random, uncontrolled posture. Parachutists generally, and the Falcons in particular, need to fight these basic instincts. Closing the eyes of course is unthinkable when they are looking for each other as soon as they exit. Their minds must be totally clear and calm and their body positions precisely controlled. Imagine *that* at the top of your tall building and you can get some idea of the sort of professionalism involved.

The result of that professionalism could be seen nearly 10,000 feet below, now, where a dozen precisely positioned Para-Commanders were drifting into their target with unerring accuracy. As far as the eye could tell, everybody got in, an impression later confirmed back at base. The winds had been fairly kind for a change and all had finally gone well.

Meanwhile, as the Falcons had been rolling up their 'chutes, the doors of the aircraft were shut and the Hercules tipped a wing to retrace its steps back to Brize Norton. It was a strange feeling to be sitting alone in a large military aeroplane. Up front, in the cockpit, the Falcons' back-up crew of pilot, co-pilot, navigator, engineer and loadmaster were expecting to be back up in the air the same afternoon with a lift of trainee paratroopers who were at that moment on the tarmac at Brize Norton nervously awaiting the arrival of the Hercules. Squadron Leader Bill Kemp in the cockpit gave the rundown on the afternoon's activities there, amidst a bewildering assortment of knobs, dials and switches.

Bill Kemp had been on his ample belly for part of the operation, since as the aircraft went close to the target, the Hercules's nose obscured both pilots' visual contact with the target. This, combined with the dense cloud cover, made it necessary to take up a prone position in the nose in order to keep visual contact through the lower windows.

Returning to Brize Norton, it became increasingly clear that the weather was closing in, visibility was poor, even at 1,000 feet, and the feeling was that there would be no jumping that afternoon. This was confirmed on landing at Brize Norton where rain was coming in almost horizontally. It didn't appear to worry the troops. When they heard parachuting was 'scrubbed' for the day, they were all smiles as they trudged back to the hangar. For them, static-line parachuting with its heavy awkward equipment and sometimes hundreds of other parachutists in the sky at the same time, held little of the appeal of the Falcons' style of parachuting. Basically, it entailed most of the minus factors involved in parachuting and few of the plus factors, namely a lack of height and time, low performance canopies, sharing the aircraft with fifty or sixty other sweating, nervous and sometimes vomiting colleagues, and a commitment to taking infantry weapons and equipment wherever they went. Not the most enviable of prospects. Now they could forget all that until another day.

The Falcons, for their part (now returned from Weston by bus) would go straight back into the hangar to re-pack 'chutes for the following day. It could have waited. In the morning, the March winds returned and everything was scrubbed for the day.

SIX

"Smile, you buggers."

As March turned to April, the weather began to pick up slightly. It was still breezy and cloudy but the clouds were higher and offered occasional clear patches. The latest intake of Territorial Army 'paras' had completed their initial ground training; the time was ripe for their first aircraft jumps and the first Monday in April saw sixty-one hardy souls assembled nervously outside the operations room at Number One Parachute Training School, Brize Norton.

They sat patiently in two rows awaiting the arrival of the aircraft from R.A.F. Lyneham. One or two were reading, apparently unconcerned and nonchalant.

"I wish I had the self-control to read and relax at a time like this," I confided to their instructor, Sergeant Brian Davis.

"Don't worry," he returned. "They've probably got the books upside down anyway."

The message came through that the aircraft would be thirty minutes late, time enough for a final exit practice from the Hercules mock-up. Far better to involve the troops in some activity rather than have them sitting about becoming tense and anxious.

From the Ops room came another message; the aircraft was on its way. "Right. 'Chutes on!" The jumpmaster's voice was urgent and there was a flurry of intense activity as sixty-one parachutes were fitted. For several minutes the only sound was the clink of harnesses as fingers fumbled nervously at chest straps and clips and quick-release boxes. Minutes later, the Hercules taxied up to the hangar with its customary roar and the troops filed out on to the tarmac. For some moments they stood in the gale-force wind created by the aircraft. It was to be an 'engines-running' emplane which allowed take-off almost immediately the troops were on board.

The jumpers made their way up the steep incline of the tailgate which had been lowered to the tarmac. The last six struggled manfully with their heavy weapon containers which they would attach to one leg prior to being called to the door. No longer first time jumpers, these six were now within one jump of the required eight before being presented with their coveted 'wings' qualifying them as military static-line parachutists. For the remaining fifty or so, however, this was a totally new experience. They sat obediently now, arms folded across their reserve ripcords protectively.

In the seat nearest the door sat the 'drifter', on this occasion Sergeant Instructor Evans, whose task it was to jump at 1,000 feet and do precisely nothing except control his landing. This gave a reliable pointer to the wind conditions and would enable the pilot to give the green light at exactly the right time over the dropping zone.

As usual, Taff Evans was in joking mood and his breezy confidence contrasted comically with the preoccupied and tight-lipped troops as the Hercules surged forward for take-off. There was the familiar elation and exhilaration as the aircraft accelerated to more than one hundred and fifty miles per hour, but the troops appeared distinctly disinterested. One or two forced a joke but elicited little response. Many were apparently asleep, again displaying that curious reaction as a defence mechanism.

Within five minutes the Hercules had levelled out at 1,000 feet and drifter Taff Evans stood up for an equipment check and to hook up his static line. Behind him and jumping with him were two DZ officers. They had the choice of travelling to the drop zone (Weston-on-the-Green) either by the R.A.F. ambulance, Land Rover or similar DZ vehicle, or they could fly there with the troops, jump with the drifter and still be on the DZ in time to supervise the landing of the troops. All three stood up now as the port door was lifted clear to the accompaniment of a vicious slipstream noise which drowned all other, threatening almost to rip the despatcher from his precarious position at the door.

It was curious to note the effect that this had on the silently watching troops awaiting their turn to jump into what was for them the unknown. A goodly number averted their gaze deliberately, studiously avoiding the reality and inevitability of their own imminent exits. Others were almost hypnotised in their fascination and stared, pop-eyed and transfixed, as the three instructors moved towards the door, calm and confident and quite unconcerned. The light at the door showed red for five seconds, turned to green and with a single step and a powerful kick away from the door they were gone, whipped away by the slipstream the moment they stepped out. The importance of that good, hard kick out of the door was soon to become very evident.

Meanwhile, the despatchers hauled in the static lines of the three who had jumped—no easy task, this, for once even a light object such as a static line or, more particularly a stick of twenty-plus static lines is pulled into the slipstream by the jumpers, it is a two-man job in many cases to heave them back into the aircraft. That accomplished, the door was closed again and relative quiet returned. The door would be opened after the aircraft had turned and was approaching the run-in for the second time.

Next out were to be the container carriers on their final jumps before receiving their wings. Just the three of them, and each had seven jumps under his belt, so the procedure was second nature although they were still very much at the nervous stage. Their training had been thorough, however, and they went out quickly and cleanly.

Now came the turn of the first-timers, looking tense but committed. The crunch had arrived and there was no going back short of refusing at the door, not a particularly unusual occurrence but unthinkable for the great majority. In any case, by the time military parachutists had reached this stage they were so conditioned to reacting instantly to the command "Go!" that to jump was an automatic response.

In the event, it was remarkable how many of these recruits were able, in the final analysis, to condition themselves to keeping their minds clear and positive at least until they were out of the door. Some were clearly elated, almost drunk with exhilaration or fear or both, suddenly extravagantly jovial. A few appeared (to quote a Forces expression) decidedly 'switched off', an impression that was to be confirmed in the next few minutes. Despatcher and instructor, Sergeant 'Miko' Mikolajewski made his way back along the lines of troops having checked out their equipment.

"Very nervous, this lot," he bent and confided in my ear. "Have you checked this, have you checked that, is this all right, is that all right?"

The door was lifted clear; again there was the shock of the chilling slipstream as Miko called his port stick of four to the door.

"Action stations!" The familiar command known to paratroopers everywhere was barely audible above the noise of the engines but that did not matter; the gesture was sufficient and four very serious-faced troops advanced falteringly as the aircraft lurched slightly in pockets of turbulent air on the run-in. Number one stood in the door, one hand on the edge to support himself. He was followed closely, too closely, by the other three and for a few brief moments there was the usual bumping and barging of one man's reserve parachute against the bulky main parachute of the man in front, setting up a sort of chain reaction all the way along the stick. Miko held on to number one's harness to steady him in the door and prevent a premature exit. He turned his head to the lights above the port door and there were a few seconds of tense inactivity as he waited for the cautionary red signal.

"Red on!" Miko bawled in number one's ear who brought his supporting hand to clasp it firmly over his reserve, looking fixedly ahead now at the horizon. An agonising five seconds later the green light showed.

"Go," Miko bawled again at number one. He went — just! His kick away from the door was a trifle diffident and he barely cleared it. Evidently a prime candidate for the dreaded 'rivet check', a term used with typical Forces humour to describe a static-line parachutist's helmet bouncing sweetly all the way along the fuselage of the aircraft through failing to exit hard enough.

Two and three were hard on number one's heels — no problem. Four, however, was hesitant. He stopped for just a fraction of a second but long enough to lose his momentum. When the push away from the door came there was nothing behind it. As the slipstream hit him he seemed to tip backwards slightly and nearly sat on the ledge before almost bouncing clear. His troubles, however, were not yet over. Just for good measure, his head went back and clouted the step before he was gone, probably none the worse for his experience but equally probably with a few twists in his rigging lines when his canopy opened to show for his mistakes.

The doors were closed and comparative calm returned whilst the aircraft circled again for Brian Davies' stick of four at the port door, a stick that went out confidently, ably assisted by Miko and Brian who made sure that their charges cleared the door safely by means of a forceful shove in the middle of the back-pack. That is not to say that trainee paratroopers are pushed out of the aircraft as is often assumed. They are helped, certainly, which sounds suspiciously as though it amounts to the same thing, but in fact if a recruit decides he is going to refuse he needs only to push both hands rigidly up against the fuselage each side of the door to become an almost immovable object. Alternatively, when the time comes to stand up, on the signal 'prepare for action', he can remain seated as an indication that he wishes to take no further part in the proceedings. In either case, the man concerned is removed from the scene of operations as quickly as possible to avoid unsettling those around him. He does not usually get a second chance although that is occasionally requested.

On this occasion, the sticks were jumping smoothly to schedule, Brian and Miko doing an impressive job of boosting morale.

"Smile, you buggers!" Miko bellowed at his stick of six jumpers as he supervised their approach to the door. A few, a very few, took him at his word and spirits were lifted.

Brian tended to be quieter but equally effective in his approach, establishing the sort of rapport with his trainees that instilled the confidence they needed.

Both Miko and Brian were fairly typical of the staff at Number One PTS in their generally outgoing approach to life. Young at heart as well as in years, there was nothing of the military stiffness about them that might be expected. On the contrary, their very human and easy-going natures always made themselves felt. Currently not as experienced as the Falcons display team as far as the number of free-fall drops they had completed was concerned, they were nonetheless the sort of rugged individuals of whom future Falcons' teams would consist. Naturally enough, the ultimate aim of many of the instructors at the school was to put in a couple of years on the team, so competition was fairly fierce. For the present, though, Miko and Brian were committed to the 'bread and butter' side of parachuting. Their dedication to it was as impressive as it was evident and they clearly loved the work, particularly at 1,000 feet with the doors off. Their only reservation was that the commitment to training troops strictly limited the number of descents they could themselves make. Their time would come. Right at this moment, their task was to complete the emptying of an aircraft that thirty minutes earlier had been claustrophobically full. The remaining troops went out in sticks of six as I stood on a seat next to the door watching the slipstream sweep them inexorably away like rag dolls, their feet suddenly thrown up towards the horizon before the opening parachute straightened them out.

The team ready to emplane, beside the tailgate of the Hercules. Left to right are: Simon Bales, Roger Nicolle, Dave Armstrong, Joe McCready, Phil Kelly, Bob Kent, Graham Pierce, John Gregor, Steve Rowe, Alistair MacDonald, Tommy Johnston and Dave Ross.

The 'Big Iron Bird' completes another low pass, this time over the American air base at Woodbridge, Suffolk.

Gloomy interior of the Hercules half an hour before display drop. Dave and Simon already kitted up and at work on windspeed calculations. Remainder of team fitting 'chutes and smokes' at the front of the aircraft. Loadmaster Stan Unwin (centre) keeping communications running smoothly.

An unusual shot from the ground using a telescope, showing exit from 3,200 feet. Note the turn outward from aircraft at ninety degrees to aircraft heading, ready for a stack pull.

Staff of Number One Parachute Training School, Brize Norton, all ready to go for a high one off the ramp.

'The Tartan Trackers', alias 'The Flying Scotsmen'. Tommy Johnston, Dave Ross and Alistair MacDonald.

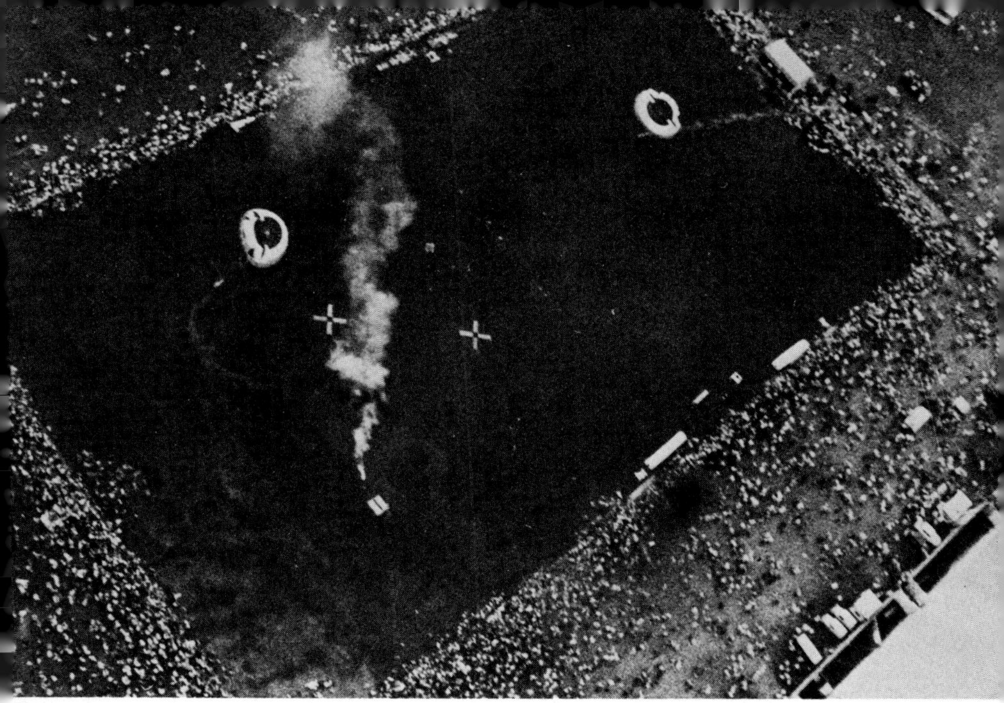

Falcons' eye view of a typical display venue. Taken from under canopy at about 1,000 feet; the target crosses, flare and windspeed indicator stand out surprisingly clearly most of the way down.

The whole team in the sky over Weston-on-the-Green. Those without smoke showing are not yet down to 1,000 feet. Top left and top right, Bob Kent and Graham Pierce have just released flag smokes which have fallen below them on a cord.

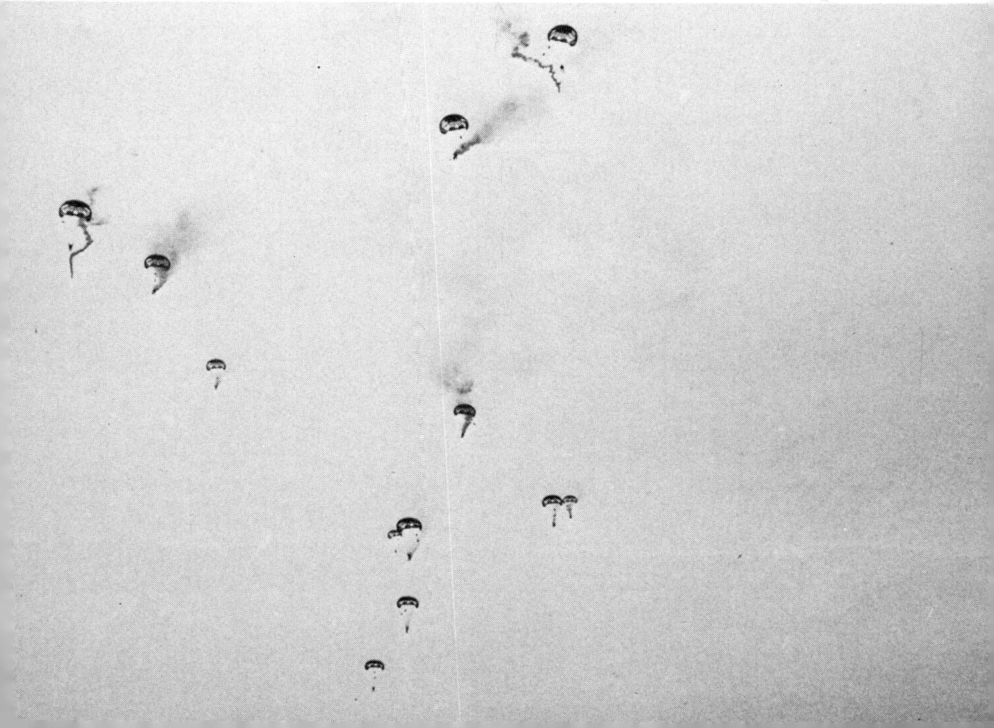

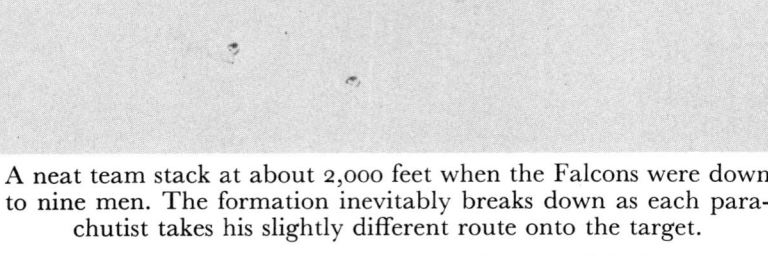

A neat team stack at about 2,000 feet when the Falcons were down to nine men. The formation inevitably breaks down as each parachutist takes his slightly different route onto the target.

John Conrad falling stable and watching the ground for his opening point. Working with hand and arm to get onto the right heading ready for the pull.

Last man out of the starboard door hits the slipstream; Steve dispatches.

The moment of exit, from outside the aircraft. The body position is completely symmetrical as the jumper goes out facing the 'prop wash' in order to remain stable in the slipstream. The next man out is hard on his heels.

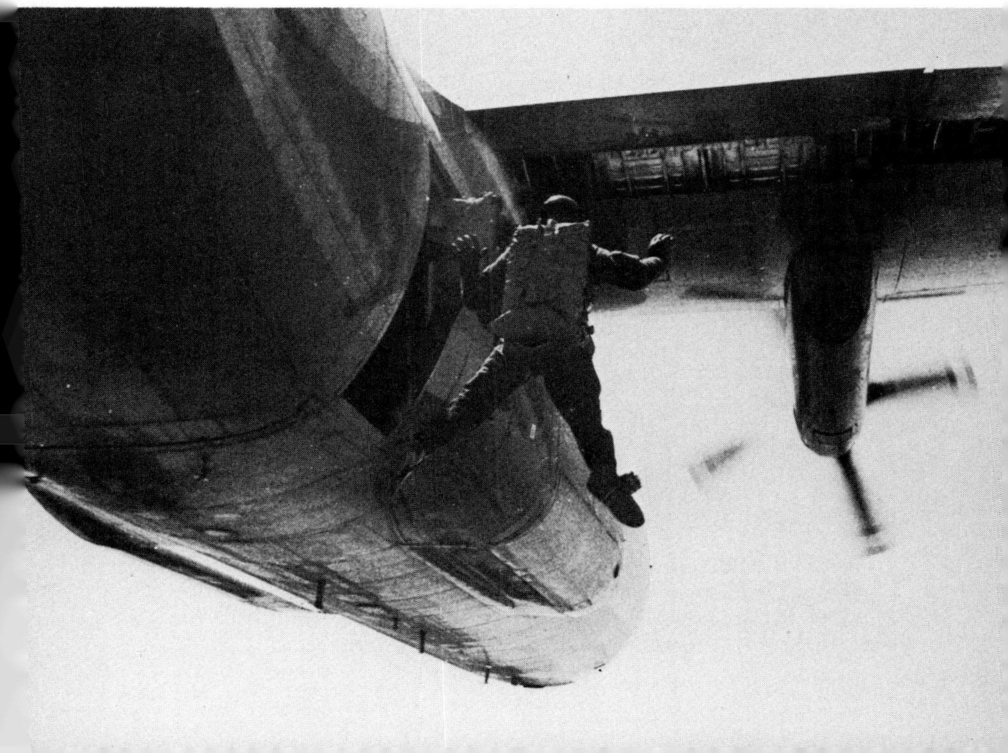

Joe McCready about to deploy his canopy 2,500 feet above Coventry. A stack pull in which he 'unpacked' as soon as he was out of the aircraft, (from which the photograph was taken). Notice how he is 'sitting up' to soften the opening shock.

The enormous interior of the Hercules seemed eerily empty after all the troops had jumped. Miko and Brian sat at the front of the aircraft with a cup of coffee. It seemed the prudent thing for me to remain at the rear — now that the excitement had died down, I had become uncomfortably aware of the somewhat erratic motion of the aircraft in the slightly turbulent conditions at low altitude. Suddenly and to my everlasting shame I felt an overpowering need to retch and lurched across to the recess set into the side of the fuselage for just such a contingency. Afterwards, I looked up to see Miko grinning broadly at the other end of the aircraft giving the thumbs-up sign. I don't believe I managed to grin back. "Don't worry about it," Brian said later, "nobody honks more than I do!"

At the crack of dawn on the following morning, the main hangar at Number One Parachute Training School was already in full swing. By 5.30, the latest intake of Territorial Army troops had drawn and fitted 'chutes ready for a 6.30 drop at Weston-on-the-Green.

At 5.45 the Falcons arrived looking resplendent in blue jump-suits in contrast to the drab, khaki camouflage of the troops. Simon immediately got into a 'hassle' at the Ops room where his team appeared to be the target for mild hostility occasionally. With characteristic diplomacy, he seemed to soothe the injured parties at Ops. That was something most apparent in Simon's make-up; whatever the situation, he always seemed to maintain an unruffled calm, doubtless a valuable asset in a job where a cool, detached decision could mean a man's life.

Soon after six o'clock that morning, a very full Hercules left the runway at Brize Norton and minutes later was over the drop zone at Weston with its cargo of T.A. trainees, one drifter, four ground party jumpers and the Falcons who were presently tucked inconspicuously away on the front seats furthest from the doors and therefore somewhat hidden from view behind the lines of troops. From where I was seated adjacent to the starboard door, only the flash of a red helmet now and again betrayed their presence. The Falcons would be remaining where they were whilst the aircraft dropped off the static-liners at 1,000 feet.

The dark, wiry and constantly wisecracking Taff Evans was again acting as drifter and was his usual ebullient self. A sweating recruit who sat opposite Taff was escaping into a last-minute sleep but Taff had other ideas. He tapped the recruit on the knee.

"Ham and tomato sandwiches O.K. for you?" he enquired innocently.

The recruit looked up, puzzled, but seconds later his chin dropped to his chest again as he dozed off. Taff roused him a second time.

"Two sugars in your coffee?" he enquired again.

The recruit remained distinctly unmoved and looked stonily at Taff until he realised he was surrounded by a sea of grinning faces. He gave up trying to sleep and studied his reserve sheepishly. The thought of a restaurant service in the aircraft at a time like this was slightly ludicrous and seemed to spread a little light relief all round. Always a great one for easing tense situations was Taff.

Meanwhile, the aircraft was approaching the dummy run-in; the drifter and ground party cheerfully made ready. There was the usual shock, like an icy, cold bath, as the doors were opened to reveal Weston shimmering and sliding by below, alarmingly close now as the Hercules tipped a wing steeply to turn in for the final approach. Seconds later, the drifter plus four were out, quickly, routinely, efficiently. The door was closed again whilst the first stick of eight Territorial Army troops made ready for their own exits, their second in consecutive days. Hopefully, they would this time be a little more aggressive in their launch into the slipstream in the few cases where this was necessary and as they went out in their sticks of eight it was clear that most had learned that lesson. Some had not, though, and five or so held back momentarily at the door and had cause to be thankful that they were wearing sturdy helmets.

The aircraft was cleared of the troops without further incident, however, leaving the Falcons to their own devices. They sat minus equipment now but as the Hercules began its ascent to 12,000 feet they donned 'chutes, smokes and helmets ready for a one minute free fall. It soon became clear that they would not be going anywhere near that height. At just 3,000 feet the aircraft hit thick, cotton-wool cloud and Simon motioned downward to indicate a low level stack pull with only a very brief delay of perhaps three seconds, known as a 'clear and pull' or alternatively as a 'hop and pop'. The doors were opened without further ado and Simon and Davie knelt with heads in the slipstream guiding the pilot to the release point. Both suddenly stood up, disconnecting their throat microphones as they did so since they would have no further use for them, and moved back from the doors, a signal to the rest of the team standing on the steep incline of the tailgate to jump. First man out on the starboard side was Graham Pierce who stepped forward now, looked across to the port door to synchronise his exit with his link-man (although on his occasion there would be no link), pulled the pin from his smoke canister, nodded and was out. His exit was hard and he seemed to clear the aircraft by several feet, turning to face the propellers as he did so. Just for a moment he seemed in some mysterious way to hang motionless in the slipstream in a symmetrical frog position before dipping his shoulder and smoothly turning away. The remaining five followed on so quickly it was impossible to observe them individually and the aircraft was suddenly very empty. Only a few hundred feet below, Graham was already reaching in for the pull and his canopy was first to show. Someone immediately behind him seemed to have a hesitation on his pilot 'chute which flapped around briefly like a mad thing without pulling the main canopy clear. It looked alarmingly like a malfunction until a violent wriggling of arms and shoulders disturbed the air sufficiently for it to catch the pilot 'chute. Last man out on the starboard side, Dave Ross gazed back up at the aircraft all the way from exit to ripcord pull, waving and grinning cheerfully the while. As the canopies blossomed four or five hundred feet below, I lay on my belly, fascinated, and watched all twelve of them descend peacefully into the pit at Weston.

The Hercules turned to make the ten-minute return journey to Brize Norton and I sat alone in the vastness of the aircraft contemplating the following year's team leader, Roger Nicolle's assertion that a job on the Falcons' display team "beats working for a living". Not many would agree with the inference that the job was in any way a sinecure; Roger used the term euphemistically. All the team, however, would very probably agree with the implication that the job was a labour of love. After what had just been witnessed, it was easy to see why.

SEVEN

Happiness is 'Chute-Shaped

The following Monday, the Falcons were aloft again over Weston. This time they had the aircraft to themselves. The chocks had been rolled away at 9.20 that morning and now minutes later the relative men took up position in the Hercules in a dry run-through of the relative work that was imminent. The team had been jumping regularly for some weeks and were beginning to iron out the wrinkles in readiness for the display season. They were relaxed and confident with little sign of the tension that had occasionally made itself felt some weeks previously.

The sun was streaming in through the doorways as the team stood poised to make their exits at 10,000 feet, John Gregor again nonchalant, almost bored; Rog Nicolle smiling happily and relishing every minute; Graham Pierce alert and professional as ever, probably at that moment running through a mental rehearsal of the five-man link-up with Phil Kelly, Joe McCready, Steve Rowe and John Gregor. The sixth relative worker, Bob Kent, was out with a cold. A condition such as a blocked nose made it medically inadvisable for him to undergo the changes in pressure that occurred at 10,000 feet.

Right on P-hour the Falcons stepped into the blue, jumping through a convenient gap in the patchy cloud over Weston, turning left and right to take up the display formation. Almost directly below the aircraft the five-man link was getting together. The last man in almost lost it as he tried to complete the link; his legs seemed to drop as he reached to grab the jumpsuit of his opposite number but he recovered immediately and the 'five-man' was complete, now little more than a dot as the Hercules circled the DZ. It was just possible to make out eleven canopies some seconds later as the relative men bomb-bursted out to their opening points and the trackers turned back in to theirs. Eleven canopies? I searched for the twelfth until I remembered Bob Kent was missing. A canopy failing to deploy would indeed have been something of a rarity. The three-year time lapse since the last malfunction was a safety record many in parachuting circles would wish was theirs. The 'spot' for the jump (that is the point of exit as decided upon by the team leader) had been good and for once there was only a moderate breeze. One by one the canopies came in on target and draped themselves lovingly across the landing pit which was soon a riot of red, white and blue. Everyone got in and the aircraft turned away on a heading for the United States Air Force base at Upper Heyford only a few minutes flying time from Weston. The Falcons, meanwhile, would bundle up the 'chutes they had just used, get on to a bus carrying their second 'chutes and ride to Upper Heyford to meet the aircraft for a second drop.

We in the aircraft should have been there long before the Falcons arrived but as we landed it was clear that they had been waiting for some time. The Hercules had spent almost half an hour circling away from Upper Heyford on orders from ground control. It was a pleasant ride 'up front', smooth and as quiet as a family saloon. It made a change to be surrounded by windows in the cockpit rather than the bare, metallic austerity of the aircraft's belly. As we taxied along the runway a jeep intercepted with lights flashing. Written on its rear in true American fashion were the words 'FOLLOW ME' in bold red letters. It seemed a curiously and amusingly inappropriate and unmilitary request for such a high-powered military base where swing-wing jets were taking off on the adjacent runway. It was effective, though, and the escort vehicle took us direct to the Falcons who climbed aboard immediately.

The second drop was to be something of a fun jump incorporating relative practice for the display trackers who would be going for two separate links of three men, whilst the display relative workers would go for another five-man link. Later in the year, Simon informed me on the ascent to (hopefully) 12,000 feet, the team would be trying for a twelve-man link. Some of them were sceptical that this was a viable proposition and indicated that the idea was possibly a trifle over-optimistic. The team just did not get enough of that sort of sustained relative work practice since nearly all of their drops centred on the display formation. When there were half a dozen or more men linking up they tended to set up a lot of turbulence in the air around them and it needed a highly skilled and specialist relative worker to break through this turbulence and get in at the right speed without upsetting the delicate balance of the circle. The general consensus was that eight or nine men in the link was a more realistic figure.

That was all in the future, however; for the present there were more immediate tasks. As the meteorological report had predicted there was a lot of cloud building up but as yet there were still plenty of gaps and as the Hercules circled Weston at 12,000 feet the DZ was only occasionally hidden from view. Steve Rowe was looking decidedly unwell and came across to breathe the oxygen available through a tube located by the door and set into the side of the aircraft. After taking a few whiffs he came and sat down heavily opposite to me, raising his closed eyes to heaven whilst the feeling of nausea passed. He would be glad to get out of the aircraft.

"Bit of anoxia," he confided when he opened his eyes a minute later. "When you take the oxygen you feel worse before you begin to feel better." He got up and made his way to the ramp and was soon joined there by the rest of the team. They were looking forward to this one, freed of the constrictions of display routine. As they looked toward the open doors there was another bonus; the sky was clear all the way down to the ground from 12,000 feet. The view was sensational, the team exit probably the most exhilarating scene I had witnessed; so much so that I was at a loss to understand the look of total disinterest on the face of the loadmaster. Ah well. Each to his own; jumping out of aeroplanes isn't everybody's cup of tea.

A matter of a few seconds out of the aircraft and the Falcons were already forming distinct and separate groups as they had planned prior to leaving the aircraft. For the first time on any drop I had witnessed, the whole team disappeared from view. They quite simply and amazingly vanished. Before, they had always been visible as dots right up to the pull of the ripcord. Now, forty or so seconds out of the aircraft, there was a good ten seconds of wondering where the hell they were. When they did reappear nearly one minute after leaving the aircraft, the fully inflated canopies were barely discernible as they headed for the pit. Nearly all of them were right on target; one obviously had no intention of going for the pit and landed on the grass over a mile away. It was strange to realise that a couple of minutes beforehand a team of parachutists had been standing larger than life where I was; now they were walking about on Mother Earth more than two miles below and all because of a few square yards of nylon material.

The loadmaster came over and pulled the door closed much to my disappointment. He still looked bored. One might have thought that the events of the last half hour were commonplace. Perhaps for him they were but for my part the senses reeled as the Hercules retraced its steps to base.

Back at Brize, 'Free Fall Training Flight' were training a new intake of military high-altitude jumpers. They would undergo an intensive period of ground work prior to going straight up to 25,000 feet, a sobering thought indeed. This sort of course, naturally enough, is not designed for the bulk of parachutists that pass through the hands of the Falcons and their colleagues. Personnel who undergo the H.A.L.O. course are carefully selected for aptitude and may be members of the famous and formidable Special Air Service, parachute school staff, troops from crack units or other such specialists. I got the distinct impression when present at some of these sessions that my presence as not as welcome as it might have been and this was confirmed when I was later strongly advised to ensure I was in the company of one of the Falcons when visiting that scene of operations. I had, evidently, inadvertently touched upon a sensitive area but it had been interesting to note the difference in approach to H.A.L.O. training. Where normal static-line troops were taught *en masse* in groups of as many as twenty or, in the case of exit training from the Hercules mock-up in two sticks of thirty, the high-altitude men remained for much of the time in fours or fives. On this occasion there were three such groups spending most of the time on their bellies in the various free-fall positions; the dart-shaped delta position which would (hopefully) maintain stability on exit, followed by the frog as soon as the slipstream had been cleared. In charge of one of the groups was the affable John Kirk who, for all his rebelliousness, was clearly as dedicated to his trade as any at the school. He loved his parachuting for its own sake; the glamour side of parachuting held little attraction for him and in that he was something of an individualist, a fact that endeared him to most of his colleagues.

Meanwhile, in the Ops room adjacent to the training hangar preparations were under way for that night's final descent by sixty static-line troops who, on completion of the night jump, would qualify for their coveted and hard-earned 'wings'. The met. check was favourable and later in the day, just as dusk was settling, the hangar again became alive to the sound of a mass fitting of parachutes. We were airborne only minutes afterwards; so soon in fact that it was still fairly light by the time the aircraft was circling the drop zone at Weston. Brian Davies and Miko were again despatching and, surprisingly, soon received word from the ground via the aircrew up front to let out the first stick. The lights of evening littered the town around the drop zone and although darkness was falling the ground was still easily visible when the doors were opened to let in the chill night air. The first stick of six were lucky; as they went out it was clear that they would be able to see the ground right up until the impact of landing. The point of the night jump, of course, is to give the parachutist experience of landing without knowing when he is going to impact, this being the main reason why the night jump is not generally liked by static-line troops.

After the first stick had gone it was decided to delay further exits for a while until dark and there followed the faintly nauseous experience of twenty minutes circling at bumpy, low altitude. It was something of a relief when the door was re-opened although some were not so sure about that; although everyone now had seven jumps under his belt, Miko said, one or two had displayed a consistent reluctance to fully commit themselves to a proper exit. Miko indicated a potential refusal on the next stick. He did not seem aware that he was under surveillance and if he had known he looked too nervous to care. I watched his exit with interest and as had been anticipated he only just got out. At one point he almost sat on the step in an understandable (depending on your point of view) desire to remain in the comparative warmth and comfort of the aircraft. But it was too late; he was past the point of no return and slid incongruously into the night, banging his helmet on the sill of the door as he went for good measure.

In contrast to all that, some showed little or no discomfort as their time approached. A chap called Lazenby in particular had seemed totally without fear from his first jump onwards and now as he stood waiting to make his way to the door, he leaned casually against the fuselage and viewed the proceedings with an air of nonchalant detachment. I was reminded of the story of the Royal Marine who had passed through the school at an earlier date. He had apparently caused some amusement in the aircraft, yawning pointedly when the red light came on and obviously bored to distraction with the whole thing. How much of that was cover was something no-one seemed sure of but I gained the very definite impression that there was some doubt as to his I.Q. being quite what it might have been.

On the subject of amusing incidents, one in particular stands head and shoulders above the rest. On one of the earlier training jumps of Territorial Army recruits, a T.A. captain on a refresher course was about to make his first static-line descent for two years. Brian and Miko were acting as despatchers and as the Hercules approached the final run-in they brought the starboard stick to the door. The captain, a rather keen type, was eager to be jumping again. In the event, he was a little too eager. He was number one in the stick and as he stood braced in the doorway, Brian and Miko held him steady by means of a firm grip on his harness, a wise precaution as it turned out. The captain was looking fixedly at the horizon, waiting for the 'go' and as the red light came on Miko bawled in his ear "Red on!" The captain, conditioned by a period of instant response to an urgent verbal command, moved to exit the aircraft in the belief that he had been given the 'go'. There then ensued a sort of aerial tug o' war as Miko and Brian, quite rightly, were determined to keep the worthy captain inside the aeroplane until the green light came on. The captain, however, would have none of it — he was equally determined to get out of the aeroplane and he began to tug and pull for all he was worth. It was two against one and he was making little progress so he changed his tactics by putting his head down and trying to run out of the door. What followed was like something out of a comedy sketch. The captain's legs were actually 'running' in his efforts to get out of the door but he wasn't getting anywhere. This went on for some seconds with Brian and Miko hauling back on his harness. The green light finally came on and the despatchers released their grip on their runaway pupil whereupon the latter, suddenly free of all restraints, found himself projected through the door for the speediest exit of the day. The remainder of the stick followed on without incident, and despatchers, loadmaster, observer and one or two troops fell about in mirth.

The night drop passed without further ado except a brief delay in the proceedings caused by what was thought to have been an injury on the ground. The consequent diversion of the drop zone ambulance meant that it was not available for the next sortie of parachutists. The injury, however, turned out to be a pulled muscle and the ambulance resumed its role on the drop zone. On reflection, it was incredible that all the tension and potential dangers of the previous two hours should result in one pulled muscle in a total of sixty-four jumpers, a record of safety and professionalism that speaks for itself.

Back on the ground, the troops clambered back on the bus back to Brize where they would talk, take a pint of ale or more and the following day would receive their 'wings'. For them, one of the most demanding periods of their lives was over. For others, it was just beginning and on the following day the latest intake made their apprehensive way to Weston for that daunting first balloon drop from 800 feet. They gathered quietly in the lee of the craft suspended menacingly above the five-man cage. It was now almost a permanent feature of the drop zone at Weston and stood like a silent, brooding sentinel, dominating the landscape and the thoughts of all those about to use it for their first parachute descents.

The trainers gathered in their sticks of four in jumping order and began fitting up. Meanwhile, the four instructors of the day were to each make a demonstration descent both to remind their pupils what was expected of them in the air and to boost the morale of their charges generally. The four made their way over to the cage, the ever relaxed Vic Last and wisecracking Taff Evans sharing a joke as they went. A single, slim metal bar was clicked into place across the doorway. The fifth man in the cage, the despatcher, leaned out, "Up eight hundred feet, four men jumping."

The winch slowly began to pay out and the cage lurched abruptly off the ground, tipping forward suddenly as it did so and threatening to pitch its contents through the door prematurely. Slowly and silently, like some bloated, lurking monster hovering above the cage, the balloon raised its cargo aloft. At each 200-foot mark, a marker on the wire attaching the balloon to the winch indicated the height it had reached. At 800 feet the winch stopped paying out and signs of movement which could clearly be seen from the ground showed that the metal bar across the door was being removed. Seconds later, the tiny figure of the first man out was visible, perched on the sill of the cage. As he left the cage his body and limbs could clearly be seen taking up position for the heart-stopping plunge whilst the static line, the rigging lines and finally the canopy itself paid out in a process that lasted possibly only three or four seconds but to the first-timers would last the proverbial lifetime.

The techniques involved in ballooning, it was clear, were very different to those used in free falling from a Hercules. Because there was no forward momentum on exit, the drop was a vertical one and of course the problem of the slipstream effect did not apply. The pre-opening drop still needed to be stable and clean, however, to ensure an unimpeded deployment of the main parachute off the trainee's back. So instead of spreading arms and legs wide as in the free-fall exit the balloon jumper took up a far more compact position with both arms folded over the reserve and feet and knees together, much the same, in fact, as in the static-line aircraft drops.

The large and ponderous PX-type 'chutes being used by the PTS instructors and their pupils on this day began to blossom with clockwork regularity. Though rather unmanoeuvrable, they are amazingly reliable, trusted and well-tried, despite an alarming opening characteristic whereby the 'breathing' canopy appears almost to close again after the initial opening before finally settling down. They do tend to let down their cargoes at a vertical speed somewhat greater than that of, for example, the Para-Commander and one rarely sees a PX jumper performing a stand-up landing, not only because the practice is forbidden to trainees and troops on the static line, but also because it is a highly skilled thing to do. On this particular afternoon, Taff Evans proceeded to make the exercise seem a ridiculously easy thing to do by accomplishing it twice in succession. Most of the troops, on the other hand, were happy enough to get up and walk away from whatever landing they could manage. Most had remembered their training well but an unfortunate few made those observing nearby to wince in sympathetic agony as they crumpled up on the grass in uncontrolled heaps. It was surprising what they could get away with mainly because, whatever else they did wrong, they all remembered to keep feet and knees tightly together.

The afternoon passed pleasantly and as each nervous first-time jumper walked over to the waiting balloon so another returned after first-jump completion looking buoyant and elated. It soon fell to my lot to accompany a trio of trainees on the silent ascent to 800 feet and as the dreaded cage tipped and lifted we watched the figures on the ground grow gradually smaller. It was quiet up there—too quiet. It was a slightly subdued quartet that finally got to jump height whilst the despatcher casually pointed out landmarks on the horizon. Good psychology, this, since it did take some of the tension from the situation. The instructor continued to talk in a deliberately calm fashion and gave his charges a final reminder of their drills. He motioned number one gently to the sill and ensured he was in the right position for exit. Quite abruptly, the terse command rang out. "Go-o-o!" It came as something of a shock after the peace of the previous few minutes but it had the desired effect and number one was out and gone probably before he realised it.

"Look up!" The despatcher shouted after his pupil as the latter fell away and he dutifully looked up to check that the deploying canopy was problem-free. The process was repeated thrice more and each time the pupil managed to look back and up at us in the cage even though his boots were for some inexplicable reason coming up to meet the horizon and even though his stomach felt as though it was being rammed hard up into his chest. It was no mean feat to be that 'switched on' for a first jump and to be aware of his surroundings in such an alien situation.

"Well brainwashed, that lot," said their sergeant instructor and despatcher as the winch began to haul in the balloon cable to lower us gently to the ground where the next lift was waiting. That seemingly flippant remark was not without an element of truth. In the detached and cold-blooded confines of the balloon cage at 800 feet, some special stimulus was essential to motivate the jumpers towards total commitment. By the time they were in the door their training had taken them to such a pitch of expectation that their minds were geared wholly toward jumping, such that it would be far more difficult to refuse than to jump.

It was a flushed and elated party that boarded the coach back to Brize Norton. They had completed the first descent and it had been easy; the next would be a piece of cake, or so it felt in the post-jump euphoria that accompanied the return journey to the camp. But come the second drop or the third drop and probably many drops after that, there would still be that familiar, unsettling queasiness in the stomach that would make them wonder if perhaps it was quite so easy after all.

EIGHT

The Season's First Display

As April came to a close, the Falcons began to put their
display drops together in earnest, in readiness for the shows
that were imminent. One such was the visit of Princess Alice,
Duchess of Gloucester, three weeks hence. The Royal visit was
naturally the subject of doubtful expectation in some quarters
where the preparatory 'admin.' and bull would weigh heaviest.
The Falcons would be the people under the microscope and all
their worst fears were confirmed when it was revealed at a
briefing that the team would be wearing the hated service
dress hats for the occasion. This particular item of headgear is
hardly the trendiest piece of clothing and is something of an
outdated, sartorial disaster, ill-becoming a leading parachute
display team. It has a large, black, shiny peak much like that
of a Grenadier Guardsman and the general feeling of the poor
unfortunates who wear it only under considerable protest is
that it looks faintly ridiculous rather than exceptionally smart.

It was easy to understand the frustration of the team when
they were told of their fate. If they were to be paraded before
royalty they might at least be presented as the professional
parachutists they were rather than a group of zombies. Even
so, the information concerning the planned dress for the visit
had its lighter side; in fact, it almost caused group hysteria in
the briefing room and the whole team fell about laughing at
the thought. Simon, sheepishly apologetic at giving out the
glad tidings, had obviously anticipated the uproar and shifted
uncomfortably in his seat, somewhat abashed and em-
barrassed. His feelings on funny hats were much the same as
the others.

"I suppose we'll have to put up with John Kirk's ribald comments," he observed ruefully.

"I don't see why—he'll be wearing one too," someone else pointed out, which was cause for further amusement.

Alistair MacDonald wondered if they could go the whole hog and wear big red noses at the same time, a suggestion that was greeted with renewed gales of mirth. John Gregor, typically scornful, was even more expressive. "I'll wear a piss-pot on my head if it makes them happy," he affirmed generously. Sid just saw the whole thing as another buggeration factor.

No matter. That event was three weeks away. For the moment, there was one more pressing display for the benefit of visiting Belgian ex-paras who felt a particular affinity with the Falcons and other instructors and parachutists at Number One PTS. Some had themselves undergone basic training with British instructors during the war years and for them the visit would be something of a march back in time. They approached a hundred in number and would gather on the drop zone at Weston-on-the-Green for a display which would last for most of the afternoon and which would include drops by static-line troops, the Free Fall Training Flight, military S.A.S. type troops with equipment and, by way of a finale, a full display-pattern drop by the Falcons themselves, their first display drop proper of the new season.

The show was scheduled for a 2 p.m. start and as the time approached the weather was looking more favourable than it had done for a long time. The clouds were high and broken whilst the winds were light and steady. Over at the landing pit the Falcons' DZ vehicle was already in position. Sid was teaching a stand-in the use of the theodolite since two ground parties would be needed whenever the team were performing a display at one venue, re-emplaning and flying straight on to the next display. This would be a fairly routine schedule over the next few months as the display season progressed.

Team manager John Conrad was in radio contact with DZ control via the portable system on his back whilst John Parry used the Land Rover radio to communicate with the aircraft as he had done at Fox Covert two months previously. John Conrad encountered the first aggravation of the afternoon—could the Falcons' DZ vehicle be removed as soon as possible so that the area could be completely clear of obstacles for the static line troops. Sid raised his eyes to heaven as the message came across from DZ control to John's radio. Perhaps it was going to be one of those 'buggeration factor' days. If they were going to get off the DZ in time they would have to be quick. The Hercules with its payload of troops was already circling purposefully overhead and would be releasing them in two minutes. The Falcons ground team made swift their exit whilst the aircraft began the run in to drop the drifter. The tiny figure was visible as he stood in the door and he exited almost directly above us to hang motionless in his harness, allowing the wind to take him where it would and thus show its strength and effect for the benefit of the troops to follow. Today it was no problem; the drifter came down at a leisurely pace and stood up gently on the grass under the PX canopy a couple of hundred yards away, leading one to the inescapable conclusion that this was Taff Evans although he was too far away to be recognised as such.

Meanwhile the Hercules had circled Weston and was now approaching the drop zone on a live run-in, the first of two at 1,000 feet. The aircraft reached its nearest point to us a little over to the east side of the DZ and suddenly the troops began cascading from both port and starboard doors, all perfectly spaced and equidistant from each other. Even so, there were problems to deal with. Two canopies from different sides of the aircraft were blown dangerously close to each other immediately upon opening. They touched and for a moment it looked as though one might foul the other until the two parachutists got to grips with the situation and steered away from each other. Yet another of the troops had twists in his rigging lines all the way down to the ground, each twist effectively making the canopy smaller and consequently increasing its rate of descent. He was still kicking his way out of the twists as he landed but he touched down softly enough and all was well.

For some reason, the second drop was a somewhat different story. Whether the wind had got up slightly or the weapons containers were making their presence felt it was hard to tell, but the descent rate was certainly much higher and there were some vicious landings on various portions of the anatomy not ideally designed for the purpose, notably the backside. One chap managed a bull's-eye and landed square on his container. Some of the containers would weigh something approaching a hundred pounds and they not only caused harder landings but also made canopy control that much more difficult. With that sort of weight on board, parachuting became less like fun and more like hard work. It was surprising how the troops all nevertheless invariably walked away from the 'hairiest' of landings seemingly none the worse for their experiences.

With all the static-line men now on the ground, the Falcons' Land Rover immediately returned to the scene to prepare for both the team display and for the H.A.L.O. jumpers of the Free Fall Training Flight. At the far end of the airfield near to the control tower, meanwhile, the Belgian visitors were eagerly awaiting yet another drop, this time by three instructors of the Adventure Training Flight which caters for R.A.F. personnel wishing to try the sport. Their little Cessna 182 was now rapidly on its way to jump height and as the engines cut at around 7,000 feet, three columns of orange smoke left the aircraft and began streaking away from each other. After plummeting for something in excess of thirty seconds, three square-shaped canopies blossomed and in almost nil-wind conditions began to trace an unusually rapid path across the sky. They were the latest 'strato-cloud' parachutes with their characteristic, flat, double-layer canopies which gave remarkable control and high performance; ideal display 'chutes in fact because of their manoeuvrability and accuracy but as yet insufficiently tried and tested over a long enough period to become the Falcons' first choice. There seemed to be something of a question mark over the opening characteristics of the strato-cloud and over its reliability; there was evidence that it tended to malfunction rather more frequently than other more established canopies and jumpers had had to cut away from it to use the reserve on a number of occasions. Even today, one of the 'strats' had given its rider a very rough opening indeed and even from where we were more than 2,000 feet below it was clear that he had been thrown violently about like a rag doll because of the sudden opening shock. Evidently, the experience had not unduly perturbed him since he landed smack on target in front of the applauding Belgian contingent and performed the gentlest of stand-up landings almost as though he were stepping out of bed.

That exercise completed, the flare for Free Fall Training Flight was set off and the arrival of the visitors was awaited at the gravel pit which was the target for the remaining drops. For some reason, they stayed where they were almost a quarter of a mile away. Obviously there had been a breakdown in communications; they would not see very much from there but it was too late to do anything about it now — the second Hercules was running in to drop eleven men from Free Fall Training Flight for a full one minute delay. All eyes strained skyward to follow the fall but few even realised that the jumpers were out until their canopies suddenly appeared a little over to the west of the airfield. They had, of course, jumped without smoke and were almost invisible to all but the sharpest eyes, something of an indication as to just how effective the H.A.L.O. method of smuggling in specialist troops really is. John Conrad's voice went out over the radio: "We have eleven good canopies." At least it certainly seemed like eleven good canopies until one of them appeared to collapse suddenly and a small figure fell away from it. Those who had witnessed the malfunction held their breath, aghast, until, after what seemed an age but was probably only two or three seconds, the figure was seen to be swinging peacefully below his reserve. He was, however, now completely at the mercy of the wind since he would have little or no control over the non-steerable reserve. It was immediately clear that he would miss the DZ literally by a mile and he quickly disappeared behind a clump of trees well away to the west. A vehicle was sent out immediately to pick him up; the chances were he was quite unharmed but there was no knowing whether or not he had hit a tree or fence or similar obstacle.

John put the new information through to DZ control: "Sorry, we appear to have only ten good canopies and one malfunction; he seems to be safely under his reserve."

The remaining ten, meanwhile, were closing in on the pit but few, if any, would make it all the way in. The 'spot' had been about three hundred yards too far to the west and they landed fairly close together but well short of the pit. Immediately, the Hercules came in for the second run to drop a second stick of six, a stick that was this time just visible in the blue haze all the way to the opening point. Around the 3,000 foot mark, the spread-eagled bodies could be seen in fascinating detail, becoming larger by the second and, it seemed, alarmingly near to the ground. At this point the vital importance of the preparation, training and equipment involved would really impress itself on anyone on the ground. One becomes acutely aware of the rapidly decreasing distance between the parachutist and the earth which is only a matter of a few seconds away. In the event of a serious malfunction of the main canopy at this stage, he has in the region of ten seconds to get a fully inflated reserve canopy above him. Seen in that light, parachuting may seem to the layman to be an unduly hazardous occupation; psychologists have suggested that its participants have some sort of death wish. Yet each day in our cars and on our roads we face situations where a three inch misjudgement of a steering wheel could result in a head-on collision at a closing speed at least as great as that of a free-faller, or where the application of brakes a second or two late at a major cross-roads would mean a vehicle standing in the path of a speeding juggernaut. Daily, our lives depend on minor adjustments and fine judgements even more critical than those required by the parachutist. The difference is, of course, the completely alien nature of the parachutist's environment which tends to make everything look perhaps more dangerous than it really is. Given stability of the body position and a correctly packed 'chute, only the hand of fate or a freak opening (or should that be non-opening?) can prevent a fully developed canopy once the ripcord has been pulled.

Such was the case on this day as an impressed group of Belgians watched from afar the six canopies, again a little too far to the west of the airfield, riding in with the wind. Their leader, Wing Commander White, coming in with the wind all the way, just made it into the pit leaving his men some distance behind and well short of the pit. He was understandably surprised and irate to find that the Belgian visitors were hundreds of yards away and would have seen the static-line drops and the Free Fall Training Flight display only in miniature. He quickly got out of his equipment and stormed over to the DZ vehicle.

"Why aren't the visitors round the bloody pit?" he fumed. The manner in which the question was delivered made it an awkward one to counter effectively and with conviction. John Conrad valiantly attempted to offer suitable explanation but was evidently on to a loser.

"That's bloody nonsense!" snorted Wingco White.

For the second time that afternoon, Sid raised his eyes in silent prayer to heaven. The buggeration factor was well to the fore this afternoon.

"Get the visitors round the bloody pit straightaway!" Wingco ordered curtly.

A couple of minutes later, the Belgians began the trek over to the pit just in time to watch the exit of seven S.A.S. troops off the ramp of the Hercules. Jumping from more than two miles up, they fell free to 2,500 feet with their assault equipment and weapons of war attached to themselves. They came down under 'T.A.P.s' (Tactical Assault Parachutes) which are slightly less advanced than the Falcons' Para-Commander and are of course less colourful. Since the S.A.S. role demands secrecy, the canopies they use are camouflaged accordingly in drab olive-type colours.

One fascinating technique in use for this display involved the releasing of heavy equipment prior to landing. Where the static-line troops had let their equipment fall beneath them (on a rope attached to their harnesses) as soon as possible after their canopies were developed, the S.A.S. kept their equipment attached to their persons until the last few seconds before landing. Presumably, this served to make canopy control easier and thus facilitate the chance of a pinpoint landing. As each man came in for his landing at about fifty feet he would appear to kick off the equipment attached to his feet by means of a strap. It then fell below him on a rope in much the same manner as the static-line troops, although how it came to be attached to his feet in the first place was something of a puzzle. One was not encouraged to ask too many questions where this élite outfit of troops was concerned, however innocent the motive. As they landed just a few yards from the edge of the pit, each in turn rolled up his 'chute and made a quick and quiet departure to leave the drop zone clear for the Falcons whose display was now imminent. It was, of course, the highlight of the afternoon's proceedings and the team's Hercules appeared overhead again within minutes of the previous landings.

Where the earlier free falls had been largely invisible, the whole of the Falcons' descent could be seen in detail as they emerged from the aeroplane with smoke 'on' and tracking hard directly overhead. The six central relative workers had their link up in good time and as they came to the end of the link they turned away as one man, arms swept back delta-fashion, to bomb-burst outwards for some seconds prior to the pull. At that point, the sky suddenly became a mass of red, white and blue as canopies popped open slightly to the west of the pit. The wind had almost died in the last half hour and the team's opening point had been only slightly short of the pit; already, it was getting decidedly crowded in the air as they homed in unerringly on the target. If they had all been at the same height, some would undoubtedly have had to turn away to land elsewhere in order to avoid fouling another's canopy; the three different opening heights allowed the whole team to go for the same target without the sky becoming dangerously overcrowded, although it did seem as though it were verging on that point already. At around 500 feet most of the Falcons were well over the pit area and were now content to remain there, no longer needing to travel across the sky but needing only to drop vertically to make the target. Obviously, the Para-Commander's forward speed of ten to twelve miles per hour must be nullified to make such a vertical drop possible when there is no opposing wind to make use of. In a case such as this, each man merely pulls down on left or right toggle which induces a succession of turns directly above the target and at the same time minimises forward speed. The technique certainly worked beautifully today and the team came in one by one for the simplest of stand-up landings bang on target. It was hectic, though. Everyone seemed to be landing at once and the DZ party had to scatter occasionally to avoid being landed upon. Everyone kept their wits about them and scanned the sky constantly until the last of the team had landed. Alistair MacDonald's canopy almost came to grief on the DZ flare adjacent to the pit.

"Watch that — — flare!" he warned as he came hammering in to the edge of the pit, threatening to drape the canopy over the still burning flare. Trevor Green quickly moved between the deflating 'chute and the fierce flame which could undoubtedly have written it off, and the crisis passed. By that time, Alistair had applied the brakes to his Para-Commander and stood up in the pit with the rest of the team. Dave Ross had approached the pit at a most peculiar angle and was oscillating awkwardly as he landed. Most parachutists would have been satisfied, in a similar situation, to fold up on impact with the pit; happy, even, to walk away unscathed. But Dave, peering intently at the ground right up to the moment that his feet touched, twisted and turned in his harness with perfect timing to meet the ground squarely on two feet and perform a stand-up landing as routinely as if he were stepping off the pavement. As one of the most experienced jumpers on the team, he had obviously learned the tricks of his trade well.

Dave Armstrong, flushed and buoyant as he climbed out of his harness, had stayed at 2,000 feet for an unusually long period. He had hit a thermal and begun to wonder if his altimeter had broken and become stuck at 2,000.

As usual on any display, the first job that the team had on landing was to form up in front of the crowd (or in this case the visitors) they were performing for. This was accomplished within seconds of the last man landing and it was interesting to watch Steve Rowe show just how speedily the operation could be completed. Whilst still circling above the pit, he had un-done his chest strap and released one side of his reserve, effectively spreading the canopy slightly wider to give a slower rate of descent in the first instance and affording himself an unimpeded view of the ground in the second. As soon as his feet touched the ground, therefore, he was able to operate the quick-release clips on his leg straps, shrug his shoulders free of the upper harness and walk away from the still deflating canopy. It had no sooner settled in the pit than he had joined the rest of the team in the line up, all now standing to at-tention (perhaps a little self-consciously) before their admiring Belgian visitors.

Those few seconds of pomp and military ceremony which bring their displays to a close is one of the few times that the Falcons betray any sign of discomfort in the public eye. They seem far more natural and relaxed waiting to hurtle earth-ward at more than 150 m.p.h. than they do standing rigidly under the close scrutiny of thousands of spectators. However, this exercise over, the team are then free to roam amongst the crowd and chat to their audience.

On this day, the performance came to a close in characteristically spectacular fashion. As the team completed their line up, Simon to the fore taking the salute, their Hercules could be seen at low level in the distance, closing remarkably rapidly for such a large and seemingly cumbersome craft. The combined power of the four engines in fact gives the Hercules a potential speed in excess of three hundred miles an hour and the pilot was evidently making full use of that potential. He was screaming in at about forty or fifty feet and would pass directly above the heads of those gathered on the drop zone. The sheer size and power of the Hercules is formidable enough when it is idling or taxiing along the runway; when it hurtles by above one's head almost, it seems, within reach of one's outstretched fingers, it is quite unforgettable. The noise rises to an ear-shattering crescendo as the aircraft reaches its closest point just a few feet above the onlookers on the ground and one can find oneself wincing involuntarily or even clapping a hand over each ear. There can be few more impressive sights or sounds and the Belgians were visibly awe-struck, watching in amazement as the huge troop transporter came to the end of its low pass to swoop suddenly skyward and into the steepest of left-hand turns that would have left many a smaller and supposedly more nimble aircraft hopelessly lost in its wake. An aerobatic Hercules was something you didn't see every day!

The Falcons returned to the canopy-strewn pit to pick up their gear and the Belgians began the walk back across the DZ to the assembly point at the airfield entrance. Here, they would present the team with a commemorative plaque of the occasion.

Sid dashed by on the way to accommodating yet another change of plan that afternoon.

"That's another buggeration factor." He paused as he ran past. "Bloody visits!" But the grin on his face told a different story. There weren't many jobs he would swop his for.

NINE

The Dreaded Nausea

The first official day of summer brought with it the first genuine and prolonged period of sunshine for weeks. It was almost as if someone had switched the summer on and it augured well for the display season that had now well and truly arrived. The only problem was the blustery winds that insisted on making their presence felt on an irritatingly high number of occasions.

Such was the case on the morning of the Norfolk display. The Falcons were to jump into the airfield at Seething later that afternoon and as they began arriving at Brize around midday it was clear that the drop would be in doubt; the winds were already on the limit and were expected to rise as the day progressed. Still, the met. report had been wrong many times before as everyone would testify.

Graham Pierce, stills photographer, was first to turn up. He arrived just as the display Hercules was taxiing to the emplaning point only a matter of a few yards away outside the hangar. We watched it for some seconds.

"I bet that starts the adrenalin flowing?" I ventured.

"Not any more," Graham replied. "But I'll start feeling it when there's about four minutes to go, certainly. I don't reckon anyone really gets completely used to jumping from a Herc. at that height."

From what I had seen thus far, I had already figured that out, but it was the first time I had heard a member of the team commit himself to that opinion. However, others were later to express a similar view.

Back in the team briefing room, the Falcons were preparing themselves and their equipment before assembling in the refreshment room from where the Hercules that awaited them could be seen undergoing final pre-take-off checks. Simon went through a quick, informal and routine briefing. The aircraft would be airborne at 1.15 for a 2.30 P-hour at Seething. The team would fit up in the aircraft at P minus thirty minutes, and Simon would give a ten-minute, four-minute and two-minute call prior to exit. The winds at Seething were already reported to be up to 25 knots at 2,000 feet so the team should be prepared for a possible aborted mission.

The formalities over, the twelve jumpers made their way out onto the tarmac to clamber up the tailgate of the Hercules. Inside the belly of the aircraft, it was today strangely bare and empty. It had been 're-roled' for display parachuting and stripped of all but the minimum number of seats. The spartan appearance did little to quell the usual surge of adrenalin as the engines were started up and their awesome power began to rock the machine to its core.

The take-off in a Hercules is always interesting to say the least. There is so much power on tap that the acceleration the plane is capable of over the first few hundred yards almost defies belief. Like most large aircraft, if one looks at the Hercules whilst it is stationary on the tarmac, it is difficult to imagine how it ever gets off the ground at all. But get off the ground it most certainly can — and with a vengeance. It is rather like the bee which, according to all the known laws and theories of flying, is physically incapable of flight. Apparently, no-one has told the bee since he obviously manages very nicely thank you.

The Herc. levelled out low at around 1,000 feet for the forty-five minute run to the display venue where five thousand expectant spectators were already being entertained by other events on the air display agenda, oblivious to the approaching team of twelve. The latter, meanwhile, were having a rough ride. There was usually turbulence on low flights but the fickle winds and weather of the past months seemed to have brought an increasing number of uncomfortable rides. Everyone felt the effects of them to some degree; the sick bags placed conveniently along the fuselage were being used on most trips. Afterwards, of course, it was a constant source of amusement to recount stories of the poor, wretched souls who had been heaving their hearts out, perhaps only a couple of minutes before exit. For the individual concerned, though, being air sick was anything but funny although he too was usually able to laugh at himself afterwards. There was always something strikingly amusing about the inevitability of it all. It was strange how it affected different members of the team at different times but it seemed that there was a distinct correlation between being air sick and boozing the night before.

John Gregor delighted in telling of the time that Dave Armstrong had succumbed to the dreaded nausea as the team stood on the ramp with a mere two to three minutes to go before exit. Dave was struggling to hold everything in until he was out of the aircraft but with a minute to go, the evidence, as it were, was beginning to show and poor Dave was forced to stand and suffer in silence as his breakfast began to creep down his chin. Exit time came and with it a merciful release as Dave threw caution to the wind and anything else that needed throwing with it. The slipstream did the rest of course and Dave discovered the truth of one of the natural laws governing parachuting, namely; "If thou art sick in the slipstream, be it upon thine own head!" Naturally, neither Dave nor his jumpsuit were a pretty sight on landing.

Now, on the flight to Norfolk, it was Simon's turn to fight the debilitating effect that air-sickness has and he went up front to join the aircrew in their slightly more comfortable, quieter and smoother surroundings. For Simon, the nausea of a rough flight was particularly unwelcome. He had his calculations to work out, information from the ground to assimilate, decisions to make and a host of other essential pre-jump items to attend to. Yet a severe bout of sickness tends to drive out all thoughts other than those of the waves of nausea and it takes considerable strength of will to carry on with the job in hand. Fortunately, Simon had a fair amount of travelling time to get it all out of his system. Then the aircraft would climb above the turbulent lower atmosphere as it came nearer to Seething and everyone would feel more comfortable.

I joined Phil Kelly gazing from the port-door window at the incredibly neat patchwork of England sliding by serenely below us. Every now and then, we would hit a thermal and suddenly lurch upwards, only to meet a downdraught and lurch equally suddenly downwards. I must have betrayed the fact that I was myself feeling decidedly queezy; Phil was grinning broadly. "This is nothing compared to one drop we did last week. Half the team seemed to be honking on that one." At least it was nice to know even the professionals disgraced themselves occasionally too.

Whenever the aircraft passed over a place of particular interest the team would be up on their feet, standing on seats to get a better view out of the window. Perhaps one should have said *most* of the team would be up on their feet, Bob Kent, as was his wont, slept most of the flight away with his helmet on, oblivious to his colleagues walking around minus all their equipment. Dave Armstrong had obviously not been too worried by his earlier bout of air-sickness; he was munching contentedly on a packet of crisps, quiet and reserved as ever but just as likely to be abruptly assertive if the situation demanded it. Steve Rowe was reading, Rog Nicolle writing; Simon had recovered and was relieving himself. Altogether a most relaxed and peaceful scene. Even the turbulence had stopped now, there wasn't a cloud in the sky and the eastern countryside was a delightful mixture of greens and browns and, most striking of all, the bright yellow of field after field of oil seed rape or kale; whatever it was, it dominated the countryside all the way from Brize, through to Peterborough, Alconbury in Huntingdonshire and Mildenhall. The U.S.A.F. base at Mildenhall was the source of much interest for one of the American Galaxy aircraft could be seen on the ground dwarfing even the mighty Boeings with it on the runway. Very soon afterwards, the landscape underwent an abrupt change as the heavily wooded area of Thetford Chase came into view. Coincidentally, the atmosphere in the aircraft changed equally abruptly. It was time to kit up, ready for the dummy run at P-hour minus twenty minutes.

Snippets of information were beginning to filter through. The wind was strong and unfavourable and would blow the team toward the crowd; that meant the only overshoot in the case of a misjudgement or a rogue wind would be amongst the spectators. It would be a difficult display and although nobody said as much, it was clearly on their minds as they studied the DZ photo with all its accompanying information on winds and directions and distances.

Seething hove to in the port window. The crowd appeared to be a mere handful, yet there were five thousand there, one of the many tricks that a height of 12,000 feet plays on one's visual judgement.

By 2 p.m. everyone had kitted up and been given the O.K. by that day's checker, Ali MacDonald. Exactly ten minutes later, the doors were lifted clear for the dummy run and there was the usual cold, hard shock to the system, the tightening in the pit of the stomach as the chill air outside burst in and the shrieking, incessant slipstream assailed the ears. No-one was showing it but more than a dozen hearts were racing as everyone crowded around the door to get a clear mental picture of the target and opening point. The dummy run over, the doors were closed and the Hercules banked away lazily to the left to line up for the run-in proper.

The DZ wind figures were coming in from the admirable John Conrad on the ground. One of the hardest-worked members of the team, John's position as team manager meant that he had neither the time nor the opportunity to jump other than very occasionally, but at least he would have the satisfaction of knowing that the information he was relaying now was absolutely vital to the success of the display. The story that his information told today, however, was hardly encouraging; a steady 15 to 18 knots (right on the limit) with occasional gusts of 21 knots. That meant a release point (or exit) a full mile away from the target and possibly an undignified landing. Still, there were a lot of people down there looking forward to the Falcons' display more than any other. Simon gave the thumbs up — they would go!

Up went the doors for the second time. A canister of orange smoke had been attached to a stake prior to emplaning and this was now let out of the starboard door. It would quickly catch the eyes of the spectators below whereas the aircraft on its own would not be easy to pick out straight away. The team began to make their way toward the ramp with five minutes to go before exit, the ever cheerful Rog Nicolle all smiles as he took up position. Graham Pierce suddenly produced from his jumpsuit a Basil Brush pilot complete with headset and microphone. Basil would accompany Graham on this jump to give him the feel of things; he would probably then do a couple of static-line training jumps before going for his first free fall with an automatic opening device. It was always hard to suppress a chuckle whenever the mascots that were adopted from time to time were put through full parachuting courses regardless of their being quite inanimate.

One last good luck at the DZ photo and Simon and Dave Ross were on their knees in port and starboard doors. The 'spot' was going to be a critical factor, as it always was of course, but more so today with a hefty wind pushing anyone who overshot into the crowd. A glance at the remaining ten standing on the steep incline of the ramp showed the intense concentration that they put into display drops, all eyes fixed on Simon at the door and everyone waiting for the thumbs up that would signal the start of the display proper. At 2.30 precisely, Dave Ross and Simon indicated their readiness to go, standing up as one, unplugging their mikes linking them with the ground and pilot, and tossing them out of the way into the belly of the aircraft. This was always something of a

A typical Falcons' 'six man' from an earlier year. The parachutist coming in on the left is just about to complete the circle. Height at this stage is probably about 8,ooo feet.

A trio from an earlier year's Falcons team. Parachutist on the left is flying in to complete the formation. Notice position of arms and legs enabling him to move forwards relative to the two already linked.

Tommy Johnston in a most stable of free fall positions. A team mate approaches fast from the rear in a slightly head-down position to make up ground. Notice Tommy's strong arch effect, giving lowest possible centre of gravity and ensuring a face-down attitude.

Rog Nicolle shows fine style as he manoeuvres himself into position for the camera of Graham Pierce. Height just below 11,000 feet.

Alistair caught in mid-flight at 10,000 feet.

Steve Rowe at 'ten grand', relaxing into a slightly flared position to slow his descent for the cameraman. The effect of the 120 m.p.h. airflow can be seen distorting the flesh around mouth and nose.

Dave Ross in his element at 8,000 feet. The bulges in the side of the helmet are not to accommodate big ears but to facilitate wearing of the helmet over the headset.

Dave Armstrong 'working big' at 8,000 feet.

Typical tracking position, known as a lazy track, giving horizontal movement and a head-down attitude. The next stage up from this is the 'max. track' which is achieved by hunching the back and shoulders and raising the buttocks slightly. This causes far more of a head-down position and an increase in both vertical and horizontal speed.

The Falcons meet Princess Alice of Gloucester on her visit to Brize Norton.

John Gregor, meditative and ready to move off the DZ after 'getting in' at the Tollerton display.

The end of another show. Dave Ross and John Gregor discuss how it went. Alistair watches the rest of the show.

Graham Pierce 'field packing' (a rapid but temporary means of stowage) after an accurate descent at Tollerton.

Packing session in the sun at R.A.F. Lyneham in preparation for the Bath drops. Alistair packing, Graham scratching.

Bob Kent and Phil Kelly having a good, early look from the port door at the Bath arena. The bulge in Bob's jumpsuit (right) is the flag and its smoke for use under the canopy.

ritual and the final act before the thumb went up. A last look at the ten on the ramp who were stooped in readiness with one hand on the string of their smoke canisters, a nod, the thumb and the first two out popped their smoke and were gone. The others were out after them within six seconds, turning so easily away from the aircraft, looking, searching, heads swivelling inwards to check positions relative to opposite numbers before sweeping their arms back delta-fashion to track out into the bomb-burst.

A dozen canopies were faintly discernible almost one minute from exit; the wind might be a problem but at least it had kept the sky cloud-free and given the team their 12,000 feet and maximum time in free fall.

The doors on the Hercules were closed and the aircraft banked at forty-five degrees preparatory to descending for a fast, low-level pass along the crowd line. On a good day, this can be timed to coincide with the Falcons' line-up but this was obviously not a good day. Graham Pierce had overshot into the crowd but managed to find a safe enough spot to land. Even so, the team had not had enough time to get together.

"Hell. We're too early, ' the pilot's voice could be heard over the headsets as we scanned the DZ from the window of the cabin 'up front', whence all had repaired for the rapid descent from 12,000 feet. "They're not ready for us."

All was not lost, however. Over the headset came the request from ground control: could the Hercules now do a slow pass since there was a gap in the display programme between the Falcons and the next event. The pilot obliged and this time the team were ready as their aircraft passed over them low and slow. The crowd was a riot of colour. They were enjoying themselves on a beautiful if windy day and they waved cheerfully as the Hercules passed almost overhead. They had also probably enjoyed seeing some of the team pile in rather spectacularly, such is the nature of non-participant spectators everywhere. However, the de-brief later in the day would tell more of that story. For the moment, it was time for the team to relax for an hour at Seething over a few beers that, with a bit of luck, would have been laid on by the organisers. Meanwhile, the Herc. would fly on to Norwich airport and there await the arrival of the team by coach since Seething did not possess the facilities for landing such monsters.

Standing on the tarmac at Norwich were the much loved Lancaster and its comparatively tiny fighter escort, the Hurricane, a line of twenty-five swastika victims emblazoned along its side. The Battle of Britain Memorial Flight were taking part in a number of air shows that day and had stopped off at Norwich before flying over for a display in Germany. One was forced to wonder what the people there would think of the display of 'kills' on the Hurricane. A couple of the pilots were flyers of the Douglas Bader era and, watching them climb into their original World War Two machines, it was suddenly and nostalgically as if one had travelled back thirty years in time; one almost expected to see a group of young men sprinting across the tarmac to their Spitfires, and to hear the 'scramble' alarm warning of 'bandits' at 20,000 feet over North Weald. The reverie was broken by the sight of the Falcons' coach arriving and making its way across the airfield to the waiting Hercules. They sat on the grass next to the aircraft.

Clearly, all had not gone well. The wind had not only been gusting right on the limit but had also been irritatingly erratic. A few of the team had got stand ups yet others had gone in too fast for comfort and had to take immediate action to avoid being dragged painfully and embarrassingly half way across the DZ in front of a few thousand people. Coupled with that, the crowd had not been the most knowledgeable in the world and the atmosphere somewhat lacking, although the ground party had assured the team that they had been received far more enthusiastically than other events, some of whom had faced almost a stony silence for their efforts.

"The only place you'll get atmosphere," pointed out Simon, "is in an arena." One was reminded of the manner in which the team had enthused about the displays the year before at Colchester Tattoo. The crowd of five thousand there was puny compared to most of the Falcons' venues, yet the atmosphere those five thousand generated in the small arena was electric. Today in the open spaces at Seething, the crowd had obviously not felt the same degree of personal involvement and this seemed to have a depressing effect on the team. The reaction of the crowd was, after all, one of the yardsticks by which they measured the success of a display. Entertainment was the name of the game and like all entertainers they needed some feedback on their performances.

Joe McCready was adamant. The jump should have been thrown away before they had left the aircraft. Piling in backwards and bouncing one's helmet on the ground a few times before setting off down the DZ behind a still inflated canopy was unprofessional, painful and risky. As one of the lighter figures in parachuting, Joe did tend to get blown across the sky more quickly than others and therefore landed with more horizontal speed on windy days; most of the team would sympathise with that, but, as they now quickly pointed out, hard landings and being dragged and other associated physical discomforts were all inevitably part of parachuting anyway. Bob Kent was slightly more specific in making that point.

"If you're not prepared to take a chance, you might as well take the brevet off your chest." None of the team would have dreamed of doing that, of course. There was no way one could ever take all the risk out of parachuting, not that one would want to even if it were possible. But Joe was insistent. If he had had a malfunction on his main 'chute, he would have been helpless under a non-steerable reserve in that wind. The assertion was perhaps a slight on Simon's judgement and team leadership and it begged a reply. Simon stood by his guns. The wind had not, after all, gone above the official maximum speed laid down for displays. The Falcons were down on the display agenda as definite participants and an awful lot of people had paid their money, most of them probably seeing the parachute display as the star turn anyway. In the final analysis, Simon pointed out, the drop going ahead as scheduled had been subject to his own discretion and the decision to take the jump had been borne out by its successful completion and the fact that a sizeable crowd had not been disappointed.

Joe wouldn't be moved. "You can see cowboys any day of the week at Weston-on-the-Green," he muttered as the team climbed back on board the Hercules. Weston was the home of the Adventure Training Flight who instructed military sport parachutists and was also a civilian centre, but the significance of the last remark was lost on the author.

Joe was normally one of the natural comedians on the team with a talent for impersonating John Wayne and certain key figures on the base at Brize. His repertoire of Irish jokes was a frequent source of amusement in the briefing room. But he took his parachuting seriously, having in excess of a thousand jumps to his credit, and was currently a four-man speed star National Champion, so he most certainly knew what he was talking about. Nevertheless, one could not help feeling that had the rest of the team had to make the 'jump or no jump' decision, most would have elected to jump.

Graham Pierce was also approaching his thousand jumps and, like Joe, was a present four-man speed star National Champion yet he took the opposite view that the jump was always 'on'. "We've done the jump and it was O.K.," he said simply. "I don't know what all the fuss is about."

The ground control Land Rover was backed up the ramp and secured in the belly for the journey back to Brize. The team, meanwhile, strapped themselves in for take-off. Now they could start to wind down and dissipate the accumulated tension of the day, Steve Rowe, Bob Kent and Sid sitting quiet and subdued, the rest discussing the day's events animatedly. Sid was getting stuck into not one but two meat pies and was oblivious to all about him. It seemed a good idea and I accepted a couple when they were offered. I was to regret it.

Everyone was in good spirits as the aircraft got under way. The pilot also was apparently in good spirits for he set about showing what the Hercules was capable of with the gayest of abandon. Seconds after take-off, the countryside seemed to be hurtling by at a rate verging on the alarming. Moreover, one did not appear to be gaining the height that was customary on take-off. Not to put too fine a point on it, the plane seemed to be stuck at about 200 feet and gathering speed by the second. For a few seconds, I had the awful impression that the controls had stuck on full throttle and that the Herc. couldn't climb. But if that was so, why was everyone (or nearly everyone) grinning like Cheshire cats?

The engines were beginning to emit a high-pitched whine and were obviously close to delivering full power. That meant something like 300 m.p.h. and we were hardly off the ground or so it seemed! I looked for signs of uneasiness amongst the team; the grins were still there but some of them had frozen a little. John Gregor was grimacing energetically as he glanced briefly out of the window at buildings and trees racing by. He wasn't mad about flying at the best of times.

People were beginning to climb up onto seats for a better view out of the window.

"Stand by. You'll start pulling G in a moment," a knowledgeable soul next to me confided. When they told me I could fly with the Falcons, nobody had said anything about this. Just as I was about to ask this knowledgeable soul his meaning, my knees for some strange reason seemed to buckle and I found myself squatting foolishly on the floor. Ah! So *that* was pulling G.

The situation was beginning to become a little clearer. We had apparently just 'beaten up' Norwich airport in the latest fully aerobatic Hercules. In reality, that had meant a low, fast pass over the airfield in a farewell salute on full revs. That had been followed by a sudden and steep climb and an ensuing G force on the plane's occupants. Those not used to the phenomenon or not expecting it were apt to find themselves

101

grovelling on the floor in a confused and disorganised heap. So that was why they had been grinning!

That crisis over, another was to follow. Those pies. They hadn't been such a good idea after all. I sat quietly and tried to be inconspicuous.

Sadly, one reaches a stage in air-sickness where one feels so desperately evil that one throws out all pretence of feeling normal. The body temperature rises rapidly and one begins to sweat copiously; the face undergoes a dramatic draining of colour as the contents of the stomach start to churn. At this point, men of iron generally wilt. Men of lesser mettle wish they were dead.

I reached for the nearest sick bag, trying to appear casual. All to no avail. Cries of glee went up all round. The sick bag had been seen. Steve Rowe at the other end of the aircraft cheered, raising an arm aloft in mock celebration then hunching himself forward in fair imitation of someone disgracing himself. I felt far too sorry for myself to join in the merriment that my condition had caused. I suppose it was some sort of come-uppance: I had laughed at others often enough in the last few months.

The aircraft was getting close to Brize — time to strap in for the landing. I was feeling too wretched to bother strapping in and managed that simple task only after about three minutes of pathetic fumbling. I looked up to a sea of grinning faces and a round of polite applause.

The Falcons are not just a top parachute display team. They are also piss-taking sods.

TEN

Win a Few, Lose a Few

The Royal visit of Princess Alice of Gloucester, when it came, was not the catastrophic upheaval some had feared. The admin. men had apparently done their homework and the exercise was completed with only a little wailing and gnashing of teeth.

In the event, the Falcons wore their jumpsuits rather than official ceremonial uniform and peaked hats and the occasion passed uneventfully enough apart from one or two minor setbacks. In rehearsal, it was said, the team had experienced some difficulty, when marching, in putting the same leg forward at the same time and in halting at the same time on the command Stop! But that was just a vicious rumour put about by people who had seen them tripping over each other and bumping into each other on the drill square!

On the day, it all passed off quite painlessly except for John Gregor calling the princess "Your Majesty," much to his own disgust and everyone else's amusement. "Trust Gregor to cock it up," he cursed himself roundly as the team returned from meeting the good lady.

On reflection, it had been a curious fortnight. One drop at Guernsey had been, of all things, fogged off. Biggin Hill had seen two at only 6,000 and 2,500 feet respectively owing to low cloud and the two at Market Rasen had culminated in Tommy Johnston performing a standard sit-up landing into the beer tent and Ali MacDonald demonstrating a tiptoe stand-up after his canopy had draped itself over a rugby post.

Now at the end of May, Tollerton was the venue and the Nottingham crowds swarmed into the display. The previous year, a crowd approaching ninety-one thousand had turned up but today's cold wind and gloomy low cloud would discourage a goodly proportion of them. Even so, it was a substantial gathering, perhaps twice that at Seething.

An hour before the Falcons were due to jump, a team of five Barnstormers dropped from an Islander aircraft, which at 2,500 feet was within an ace of disappearing into menacing cloud. They then managed to spread themselves about generously all over the airfield which did not augur well for the Falcons.

At the DZ Land Rover, the ground party were juggling with wind speeds and directions and losing the helium balloons at 1,800 feet in the sort of cloud one might reasonably expect in a bad November. The drop was scheduled for 3 p.m. and at 2.25 the Hercules could be seen flying around a couple of miles to the north. It had flown in from the military air base at Mildenhall where the team had been due to drop earlier in the day but the descent had been cancelled for the same reason that Tollerton was now doubtful.

Then, ten minutes before P-hour, the message everyone had been waiting for came through. The target was visible from the aircraft at 2,500 feet and the team stack pull would be on from that height. But as the Herc. came in for the dummy run over the flare, it was disapearing periodically in the cloud. Three minutes later on the run-in proper it had been forced down to an almost rock bottom 2,300. Twelve hundred yards late of the flare, the Falcons appeared in the sombre, overcast sky in two neat lines of six. The smoke had no sooner begun issuing from their canisters than canopies began appearing, precisely and evenly spaced. But for most, their luck wasn't in. They would nearly all be short of the target — quite a bit short by the look of it. Like the contrary bitch she frequently was, the wind eased off to a mere breeze. The team would have very little behind them to push them into the target even though they were perfectly lined up with what wind there was.

The first few out of the aircraft might just make it to the crowd's side of the runway. Then suddenly, the ground level winds seemed to catch a few canopies and whisk them in on target or as near as dammit. Half a dozen canopies seemed to come from nowhere and the target cross suddenly became a dangerous place to be. Everything happened so quickly it was difficult to tell who had landed where. John Gregor had got in. So too had Graham Pierce. Dave Armstrong was there. Alistair was there — just! He had landed inches away from the tarmac runway and had to land slightly with the wind to get on to the grass. He landed harder than he would have wished and was deposited on to his rear. Just so that his cup of joy might runneth over, his canopy stayed inflated and he looked set for a horizontal trip across the airfield, until fate smiled on him for the first time on that jump and his 'chute spilled enough air to collapse just feet from the flare. Alistair seemed to have a thing about flares — he had landed in similar circumstances in the display put on for the Belgians at Weston. But despite being as near to the cross as anybody, Alistair was far from pleased with the drop; in fact he was singularly depressed by it, more for the rest of the team than for himself. Some had landed perhaps two hundred yards short of the crowd line and none of the team enjoyed disappointing their audience. But the crowd had obviously loved every minute. Crowds are rarely knowledgeable about parachuting and for all they knew they might just have witnessed a display that had gone exactly as planned.

Amazingly, the canny Dave Ross had also got in and stood up under his canopy, just as cool as you like, right on target. He would have been last out of the aircraft with Simon and therefore jumped further away from the target than anyone else, yet here he was. What had happened was that he had pulled the second he was clear of the aircraft where most of the team had given it perhaps three or four seconds and lost valuable height with which to make ground. Dave had in fact had a small problem on opening. He had found himself in twists and unable to steer away from Joe McCready who was uncomfortably close at 2,000 feet. But that problem resolved,

Dave had taken advantage of his light build to skim across the sky somewhat more quickly than his colleagues.

Simon had landed on the far side of the airfield with the others who had not made it across the runway. Rog Nicolle was similarly misplaced. He had had a hesitation on his canopy before it had opened and had consequently fallen below his team mates, leaving him with less time under the canopy to make up ground.

The drop completed, Pierce and Gregor appeared to have got themselves firmly ensconced amongst the crowd, chatting and enjoying a post-jump cigarette. There was no doubt that the team radiated a certain charismatic glamour on displays; the admiring glances of some of the more eligible ladies in the crowd was testimony enough to that. But today, they wouldn't be around long enough to enjoy it — the coach had arrived to take them to a Lincolnshire air base where they would re-emplane the Hercules for the return journey to Brize.

The May display period had not been the most memorable of times for the Falcons. They had been plagued by diabolical jump conditions for much of the time and they looked for something better from June. The June schedule opened with the Bath Show at Shepton Mallet and with it, at last, an easing off of the pace. The Falcons would be jumping a total of three times into the arena on the Wednesday, Thursday and Friday at about 6 p.m. on each occasion. That meant time to themselves until four o'clock or thereabouts, time to unwind from the recent hectic pace and spate of heavy jumping. They would be based at Lyneham, home of the R.A.F. Hercules, for the duration of the Bath displays since, as they would not be able to re-emplane from the drop zone, the ensuing coach journey back to Lyneham would be less tedious than one to Brize Norton.

The Lyneham perimeter track is an impressive sight with its rows of Hercules, each row hundreds of yards long, parked wing tip to wing tip. Whatever other problems might rear their heads at Lyneham, there would certainly be no problem over aircraft availability. Problems of another sort would be inevitable, though. Every venue, every display even, had them to some degree; Lyneham and Bath would be no exception. Steve Rowe and Joe McCready were both out, mysteriously, with colds, so the relative group would be missing two of its most experienced men. Their absence for the Bath jumps was not just a minor safeguard — Joe already had a rupture in his eardrum through going to 12,000 feet with a head cold and finding himself unable to clear his ears. Steve, too, was familiar with this experience, a painful and alarming one, but his eardrums had remained intact. Now both men were grounded for a few days and could relax without the usual display pressures, albeit a reluctant and enforced relaxation, spent uncharacteristically quietly.

The remainder of the team spent much of the day, prior to jumping, on the tennis court, like Tommy, Graham, Phil and John Gregor, or alternately strolling and reading the papers like Dave Ross, or improving their golf swing like Dave Armstrong or hibernating like Bob Kent. Whatever they did, they needed the time to themselves. They had had weeks, almost without a break, of early mornings, pre-dawn preparations for training jumps and more recently an intensive period of display jumping. In theory, the three jumps at Bath would be something of a 'jolly'. In fact, they turned out to be three of the most difficult descents that the team would have all season. The arena itself was not so much the problem. It was those infernal, blustery winds that had been blowing for months. At Bath, the wind problem was compounded by the fact that it was so erratic and unpredictable. Simon was giving the 'go' on the basis of the set of figures sent up to him from the ground which were themselves the result of the theodolite readings. Yet on the first jump, the whole team had found themselves going backwards under the canopy and struggling to get into the arena. Normally, they would expect to run with the wind and facing the target before turning into wind for the landing.

The reason for the apparent discrepancy between projected and actual wind conditions lay in the presence of a hill adjacent to the arena. This must have been creating all sorts of unexpected and very localised wind aberrations in and around the arena, to the extent of it veering suddenly round to blow in two different directions on the one descent. There is, of course, no way of predicting or allowing for that sort of problem.

Additionally, Sid, Trevor and John Conrad on the ground would be sending up wind speed and direction figures based on the helium-filled balloon's flight from the target to wherever the wind sent it. The path that the team's canopies would take would be on the opposite side of the target to that taken by the balloon. In other words, strictly speaking, the best that the balloon could do was measure wind conditions in a different part of the sky to that of the parachutists. Normally, the effects of this were negligible but on the rare occasions that there were differing conditions within the space of a few hundred yards it could mean the difference between landing on target or overshooting or undershooting into the crowd or some similarly undesirable obstacle.

After the first jump at Bath, the team were very much on their guard. Twenty knots had been the forecast. Twelve knots had been the P-hour DZ figure — reasonable enough as long as it did not keep changing direction.

Over the drop zone at 12,000 feet the arena stood out beautifully as the evening sun's rays bounced off the wind-screens of the thousands of cars parked only yards from the crosses. As usual, the crowd looked deceptively meagre from the aircraft but the Bath Show regularly attracts ten to fifteen thousand people on each of its three days.

Rog Nicolle particularly was looking for a better drop on this, the second day. His first, the day before, had hardly filled his cup of joy to overflowing. He had spent much of the in-flight time trotting to the Hercules's makeshift and somewhat primitive loo and hastily pulling the curtain round to commune with nature. Flying to a display was not the ideal time to be hit by a stomach bug. At least the rest of the team could be thankful Graham Pierce didn't have the bug—he never used to bother with the curtain, much to the combined horror and amusement of those in the proximity.

Everyone had had problems on that first jump into Bath. Rog had had more than most and failed to make the target; moreover, he had landed in an area of grass used extensively by local cattle who fed on the lush, green pasture. They were consequently singularly regular in their habits and one of the worthy animals gave an impressive demonstration of this fact straight into Roger's helmet as he removed his gear on landing. On reflection, he seemed to have been 'right in it' for most of the day and looked for a change in his fortune; but, going by the reports coming up from the ground, that was unlikely. The first gave a 12,000 feet figure of 30 knots, then minutes later one of 4 knots all the way to the ground. Simon and Dave Ross, who were receiving the information as usual via their headsets, looked across at each other from their seats adjacent to the doors and shook their heads disbelievingly. They knew the winds here were erratic but 30 knots to 4 knots in a couple of minutes—that was ridiculous. They sat tight, quietly awaiting the next set of figures from John Conrad two miles below. This time it was a steady 14 knots—that sounded much more like it, and Dave and Simon got to work on the photograph of the Bath Show arena, marking on it the point over which they would exit and the opening point as well as the wind situation at regular intervals from 12,000 feet right down to the ground.

Seconds later, they were in their familiar kneeling positions at the door watching the arena glide by below them. They would need to overfly the flare by something like half a mile and let the wind push them into the target. And so, a little less than half a minute after reaching the target, ten Falcons leapt into the evening sky, incredibly clear, pure and blue now after the gloomy half-light inside the Hercules.

109

Strange how this moment never lost any of its magic. It didn't matter how many times one was witness to the moment of exit, there was always that same elation and exhilaration and coursing of adrenalin through the blood. So much so that it was sad to look at the now empty ramp and realise that it was suddenly all over and one had been left alone in the aircraft. It left a very empty feeling as though one were missing out on one of life's special experiences.

Watching the team on the ramp, with the doors open, the ground so very far below and the awesome slipstream clamouring to hurl those who entered it violently out of control, one's immediate reaction was to think, "Christ, this is a dangerous and frightening way to make a living." But now, seconds afterwards, watching the team working in that slipstream, using it to fly themselves into a different part of the sky, it didn't seem at all dangerous. They were so obviously relaxed and at home in the sky, the whole exercise seemed the most natural thing in the world. It had a certain control and polish about it that few, if any, display team in the world could match. One might reasonably have expected to grow accustomed to the performances the more that one was witness to them. In fact, the reverse was true in that one only gradually began to get a truer impression of the sheer professionalism involved the more performances that one saw. I found the twenty-first jump an even more impressive sight than the first. My only regret was that there was no other outsider on board the aircraft to share it with, since obtaining appropriate clearances to accompany the team is not the easiest thing in the world for those not professionally involved in some way. Consequently, the team rarely have many, or indeed any observers inside the aircraft when they are jumping.

Now, as the team fell away from the door, I sat in the seat adjacent and tried to get pictures of the moment of exit, hoping to freeze that fraction of a second when a parachutist is clear of the door but has not yet been ripped away by the slipstream. It was surprisingly difficult. No sooner was he in the viewfinder than he was gone and one had perhaps considerably less than half a second to catch him at exit.

With the team gone, loadmaster for all three Bath jumps, Sergeant 'Stan' Unwin lost no time in bringing the doors down again. The Herc. was being taken down in a hurry to 300 feet which necessitated all on board moving forward to the flight deck for the steep descent. Stan and I lurched forward to the front of the already nose-diving aircraft and climbed up into the goldfish bowl-like compartment where the pilots, navigator and engineer worked surrounded by dials, knobs and switches and with a spectacular, panoramic view of the sky around them. Stan ushered me forward to a space by the side window in the somewhat congested cabin and motioned me to hold on to a couple of strong points as the Hercules banked steeply ready for the run in over the team's heads. It proved to be a wise precaution since I found myself staring along the length of the impressive Hercules wing towards a point on the ground somewhat closer than was healthy for my taste. But the feelings of apprehension were as pointless as they were inevitable; the aircrew were 'Special Forces' personnel, amongst the best in the business. The casual, nonchalant way they handled such a heavy troop transporter seemed almost careless yet it was of course just the confidence and knowledge gained over the years that made it all so easy. They knew exactly what the aeroplane's limits were and stayed within them, yet to one without their many hours of flying time, it would often feel and look as though a wing tip was within feet of ploughing up some field below and that the whole craft was within an ace of falling out of the sky. All strange, sensory illusions which the pilot and captain of the aircraft, Chris Hayson, was well accustomed to.

The Hercules had an amazing way of responding to its controls. On a tight turn to the left, for example, I would watch Chris casually flick the controls over to the left much in the manner of a car being driven round a corner. The controls would then be returned to their original position almost straightaway. Meanwhile, it seemed to take some seconds for the aircraft to react fully, so that by the time it had responded to the controls there had been a sort of delayed reaction, perhaps a two-second time lapse between moving the controls and completion of the manoeuvre.

Now at the end of the turn and at minimum permitted height for display run-ins it was clear that Chris's timing was spot on for a low-level run over the Falcons' heads. As Chris and Stan and the rest of the aircrew eased forward for a better view of the Bath arena which was beginning to disappear beneath the nose of the aircraft, we could see a host of canopies fairly close together in the middle of the arena. Only a few yards away, the team were just completing the line up ready to take the salute. The jump had gone well and most, if not all of the team, had obviously got in.

We passed over the sea of thousands of faces gazing up at the speeding Hercules. Then it was time for the sudden climb away from the arena at the end of the run in and I could feel my knees buckling as the aircraft began to pull something in the region of 2g. One could almost feel the blood draining out of the upper body. Certainly, the arms suddenly felt impossibly heavy. Much more of that and one could find oneself grovelling and undignified on the floor.

The return flight to Lyneham passed uneventfully as the charming and obliging Stan handed coffees round. A well known and popular figure, Stan was to act as loadmaster for the Falcons during the next half dozen or so display jumps and his tall frame was always a welcome sight on the Falcons' flights. He seemed to love his job and knew it inside out. He and Chris Hayson's aircrew were turning out to be a good team, Stan's humour and ready smile making him popular with the Falcons, and Chris and his crew's efficiency and timing making the best of the difficult Bath conditions.

Later that evening, the Falcons arrived back at Lyneham in their coach to relax over the evening meal. They were agreed that the descent was the most difficult they had had as a team. Incredibly, the winds had been even more inconsistent and erratic than on the first jump and everyone had experienced difficulty making the arena. Most had made it, it transpired, but Rog Nicolle's run of bad luck continued and he was forced to turn away from the target to avoid obstacles, landing well out of the arena as a result.

Most of the team confessed to being shattered after the meal and wandered off to shower and fall into bed. Graham Pierce, John Gregor and Roger (who was still as cheerful as ever despite everything) decided to sample the delights of the area and repaired to a nearby hostelry where someone, either by mistake or design, promptly seized Roger's freshly-poured pint and it was never seen again. It didn't seem to be Roger's week.

As the local closed sharp at 10.30, it was agreed to make a brief call at the Lyneham Sergeants' Mess, where the bar was on late licence, before turning in for the night. Whilst seated there enjoying a quiet drink, a surreptitious arm suddenly appeared around Graham's shoulders. The owner of the arm stooped and crooned sweetly in Graham's ear. "Mind if I have a word with you outside, Graham?" The tone was too sugary and conciliatory for comfort. I had a strong feeling that the sugary one was about to display some sort of officiousness or pompous indignation. Strange how one can usually tell the type. Graham got up silently, puzzled, and disappeared for a couple of minutes outside.

"I've come across him before," John recalled. "He was a Flight Sergeant P.J.I. at Brize. Seems to have some sort of personality disorder. He came into the bar one evening at PTS when I was with my wife and didn't know him from Adam. Started making facetious remarks about me seeing other women in there. I told him, Look mate, I don't know what your game is, but if you don't get out of here . . ."

Suffice it to say that John was not a man to trifle with when he was aroused and I imagined that this strange individual had wished the Earth might swallow him up. He wasn't alone in wishing that!

Meanwhile, Graham had returned and sat down looking angry and frustrated. The Flight Sergeant had enquired if Roger was an officer. "Get him out!" he had hissed when he learned that indeed he was. Officially, the rules prevented an officer from drinking in the Sergeants' Mess unless as a guest of a member who had obtained prior permission. But rarely was anyone small-minded enough to actively take it upon himself to insist on the strict observance of this strange custom. The fellow was evidently anti-officer, a hostility which was apparently the result partly of jealousy, partly of inverted snobbery.

Roger drained his glass and got up to go. It definitely wasn't his week. His luck had to change soon.

After he had gone, Graham and John sat smouldering for some moments. Roger was well liked as a man and a colleague and easily put aside his rank. It was annoying that a fellow N.C.O. with a chip on his shoulder could put the damper on that.

The arm suddenly appeared again and draped itself around Graham's shoulders. Graham cringed in distaste. John winced in sympathy.

"Sorry if that caused you a bit of embarrassment, Graham old chap. Can I buy you a drink?"

"No thanks," said Graham pointedly through clenched teeth. The arm disappeared, which was just as well. Graham was beginning to look as though he might lose his temper. He wasn't big by any means, but he was stocky with the powerful arms of an expert gymnast.

He got up to go abruptly. "I'd better get out of here before I go over and drop that b — —." He went out into the night. It occurred to me that it was as well that the team had been jumping regularly lately—otherwise the story might have had a rather different ending.

Next day after lunch, the team gathered to pack their 'chutes ready for the third and final Bath jump that evening at six. It was another gloriously sunny day and the wind had died to a whisper. But all were on their guard against being over-optimistic. They were still concerned about those crazy winds that were so unpredictable over the arena, threatening to put them into the crowd or on top of a stand or through a car windscreen. For once, though, all the fears were ground-less. The whole show went like a dream. Even Roger's luck took a turn for the better; he landed right on the button. The winds had behaved themselves and the timing of the aircrew was immaculate. The low pass revealed all twelve of the team ready and waiting on the ground for the fly-past, their canopies littered much closer together this time around the target crosses.

Chris Hayson's young co-pilot had taken the Herc. down for the low pass and one couldn't help thinking that the turns were even tighter than before, the descent even steeper. One won-dered just how much G force the aircraft would take if pushed, so difficult was it to become accustomed to the sort of per-formance that the Herc. was capable of. Sitting down as the aircrew all were, there was not the same sort of gut-wrenching as though all the blood were being squeezed out of the stomach. Even so, Chris jokingly remarked to his co-pilot after the return flight to Lyneham, "Those tight turns were damned uncomfortable. I've got two years to do in the R.A.F. and I don't want to be killed by a silly bloody aeroplane." He sat back comfortably in the coach taking the crew back to base and blew clouds of smoke from a freshly lit cigar. It was encouraging to hear that he too had suffered slightly although he certainly had not shown any reaction in the aircraft. So it had been a little 'hairy' after all. I was glad that it had not just been my own imagination running riot.

The coach stopped and everyone dismounted to go their separate ways home. A couple of days later, the same aircrew would all be working together again, this time over Lin-colnshire where the Falcons were dropping into air displays at Coningsby and Boston.

The Sunday after the Bath displays, the weather broke. It was cloudy, cold and dismal. But that didn't appear to have deterred the people of Lincolnshire. They swarmed to the R.A.F. station at Coningsby in their thousands for the Open Day and air display taking place there.

The Falcons were due to drop at 14.40 and Sid, Trevor and John Conrad drove the Land Rover on to the DZ an hour beforehand to set up their equipment. Joe McCready too was there, still suffering from the cold that was preventing him from getting airborne.

The Red Arrows were aloft and doing their stuff directly overhead as the DZ party made their preparations. The little Gnat jets were restricted to performing their manoeuvres well in front of the crowd line in case of accident. But in the middle of the airfield where Sid was putting flares out ready, they screamed past only feet over our heads, enveloping us with their acrid smoke. There was no doubt that there was a certain magic about the Arrows. Fortunately, it was a different sort of magic to that of the Falcons so the two tended to complement each other rather than clash.

Over by the Land Rover, Sid was losing sight of the balloon well below the 2,500 foot mark which was the official absolute minimum for the team's stack pull. Twenty minutes before P-hour, the cloud was down to 1,800 feet and there didn't appear to be a break in it anywhere. The Arrows were doing their low-level display and the dark, overcast skies could take nothing away from the spectacle that they provided. But where the Red Arrows could fly quite happily at low level, the Falcons could make no such contingency plans and were not now expected to drop. True, they could theoretically jump from 1,000 feet or less and land on target quite easily; but what they had to allow for of course was the possibility, however unlikely, of the main 'chute not functioning. The ensuing cutaway from the bad canopy and consequent deployment of the reserve would require several hundred feet depending on how fast the parachutist was falling and how quickly he got to work.

Then, as seemed to have happened many times before, the sky suddenly cleared enough to change the face of the whole situation. It was quite uncanny how often that had happened in the last moments prior to important jumps. Even stranger, outside the perimeter of the airfield the cloud was as low and as thick as before, but directly above us was a considerable area of blue. So dramatic was the change that the Red Arrows quickly changed to their high level display and shot up into the patch of blue ready for the dive down into their bomb-burst, that spectacular manoeuvre that invariably brings their shows to a close.

John Conrad, meanwhile, made his way over to the control tower which today would also serve as the commentary box. The Hercules had already made one dummy pass and was now only three or four miles away to the front of the crowd line and was beginning the live run in. The decision on the height from which the jump would be made had been taken fifteen minutes earlier when the clouds had been well down below 2,000 feet; they would try for 2,500 in case there was a last minute break in the clouds, failing which they would go reluctantly home. In fact, this proved to be the right decision for although five minutes earlier the Falcons could have gone to 12,000 feet in that little patch of blue, the present maximum was back down to 2,500 feet. As the Herc. began to run in from the far side of the airfield it was occasionally obscured somewhat in the dull, grey 'clag'. Evidently, it was not sufficient to hide the now-blazing flare on the ground from Simon and Dave Ross, for about six to seven hundred yards late of the flares out popped ten little figures into the murky sky, their pilot 'chutes just visible as they pulled their ripcords the moment they were out in the slipstream. (This shortest of delays used for trainees and inclement weather is known variously as the 'hop and pop' or 'clear and pull'.)

With the whole team already under canopy, the smokes had barely had time to begin issuing their contents and most of the team landed with the bright red smoke still billowing from their boots. The 'spot' had been good. The descent had been a fairly straightforward matter of running with the wind for most of the way and a turn into wind for the landing. A bit of sideways crabbing early in the descent had put everyone just about on the wind line for the run in but Tommy Johnston had lost a lot of height with twists in his rigging lines. They had robbed him of his steering for some seconds, effectively increased his downward speed for a short period and taken him nearly half a minute to kick out of; all of which added up to a loss of some two or three hundred yards in horizontal distance, the same distance that Tommy was short of the target. He had to sprint across the airfield to join the team line up for the Hercules low pass and as he did so the smoke was still seen to be belching from his right foot with unbridled ferocity, a curious and rather comical effect.

The salute taken, a final wave to the applauding crowd, a rapid bundling up of 'chutes and the Falcons were back on the aircraft within ten minutes of having left it. Moments later, they were in the air for a second time on the way to Boston for a carnival being held there. The venue was perhaps only ten minutes flying time away but it quickly became clear that this was going to be one of the dreaded, uncomfortable, low-level journeys, always on the fringe of low cloud.

Conditions at Boston were no better than they had been at Coningsby. As the team changed their old smoke canisters for new ones in the aircraft, they would occasionally peer out of a window into the gloom for signs of an improvement but there would be none. Just the same, marginal cloud base and greyness all around. But remarkably, half of the town of Boston seemed to have turned up on the drop zone; they were arranged in a perfect square around it and even from 2,500 feet appeared a deep and substantial gathering.

The team's second 'chutes had all been packed and ready on the aircraft when they had emplaned for the second time at Coningsby, and now just a few minutes later, the Falcons were kitted up ready for the next jump.

As the Hercules circled the two crosses in the arena below, the doors were taken off to reveal an even more forbidding and awe-inspiring sight than usual. The town of Boston seemed uncomfortably close from 2,500 feet after the recent run of high-altitude drops. Not only that, there was cold, grey, clammy cloud whipping by occasionally. When the Hercules tipped its wings to turn in for the dummy run, one almost felt that one could reach out through the clouds to touch the roof tops sliding by below.

Dave Ross already had his head out for an early look at the target. Then he brought it back in and looked up, grinning cheerfully.

"Looks as though we'll go out right over the — — steeple!" he exclaimed, which conjured up all sorts of images of some hapless parachutist landing astride the Boston Stump now directly below us. Not a pleasant thought.

Two minutes to P-hour and everyone was ready to go but now contact had been lost with the ground.

"DZ 4566." The voice of the pilot came over on the intercom as he tried to call up John Conrad on the ground. He and the remainder of the ground party had left Coningsby immediately after the drop there and flown across to Boston by Puma helicopter. They had originally intended attempting the journey in the Land Rover, with police escort if necessary to clear the way. But the police had indicated that on this particular day there would be so much traffic about that they could not possibly make it to Boston in the half hour that was available. A helicopter was the only alternative.

The ground-air communications were not always what they might have been and it was ten minutes before John's voice came through loud and clear to confirm that everything was 'go' on the DZ. The Falcons were on the ramp immediately, adjusting goggles, checking altimeter readings, each with his own idiosyncratic little repertoire of pre-jump checks, checks that in all probability had already been made two or three

119

times but were nonetheless vital for all that. It brought to mind the experience that John Gregor once had of routinely checking his leg straps moments before exit, to find that both had somehow come unclipped; it had been a small, crowded aircraft and he had been kneeling awkwardly in a position that had made this unusual incident possible. Horror-struck, he understandably lost no time in refitting the leg strap clips and heaved a sigh of relief. The significance of losing the leg straps, of course, is that once they have gone there is really nothing to stop one losing everything; main 'chute, reserve, harness—the lot! The tendency of the body to continue falling at the same rate whilst the equipment was suddenly decelerating on canopy deployment would probably have resulted in John sliding out of his harness, at which point no amount of technical expertise or emergency procedure would be the slightest use. These days, John always checked his leg straps before jumping!

But now all the checking was over. Dave and Simon had been peering through the murk at the Boston DZ—now they stood up suddenly and with that familiar gesture threw their microphone leads into the body of the plane, nodded and gave the thumbs up. This was the signal for Graham in the starboard door and Bob in the port door to step forward, look in towards each other, nod to synchronise their exits, pull their 'smokes' and get out before the smoke started showing. That would start the avalanche and those few, brief, hectic and climactic seconds of total commitment as body after body piled out of the aircraft like things possessed. It was all so routine now, almost a ritual that had been performed countless times before. Yet still it never palled, still it sent the pulse rate soaring and put fire in the belly.

And then they were gone. The Hercules went into a layer of cloud and all was lost to view. Stan pulled the doors down and the anticlimax was complete. He went forward and joined Chris Hayson and his aircrew on the flight deck, and the aircraft turned back on a heading for Coningsby. Here, it would land and await the return of the team by coach from Boston; that is, it would land when circumstances at Coningsby permitted since the display there was still in full swing and the Herc. had to await clearance to land. Meanwhile, and to my chagrin, it passed the time by making endless low-level circuits some distance away from Coningsby. After half an hour, the inevitable happened and I could feel the sweat suddenly starting to break out, always a sure sign that the stomach was about to rebel.

"Oh Christ! Not again," I thought, lurching out of my seat in search of a 'Bag, Air Sickness For The Use Of'. Normally, they were all over the place when you didn't need them. Now, there was not a sign of one anywhere. Ah well. There was always the in-flight loo in cases of extreme urgency, and at least there was no-one around to witness this most humbling of experiences.

Five minutes later, I looked up to see Stan with large, humorous grin at the other end of the aircraft. He had come down from the flight deck to check on his 'load'. His timing had been perfect; his load had been rather less than perfect.

ELEVEN

A Touch of Midsummer Madness

The summer was beginning to take its toll in terms of cancelled displays. At the season's half way mark, half a dozen shows had been lost through the diabolical conditions and many more had been minimum height jobs. Even so, the picture could have been far worse had not the team had the elements on their side at crucial moments.

On other occasions, unusual conditions had played almost unbelievable tricks with people's canopies. The Paris Air Show drops midway through the season were the most remarkable to date. In front of the usual colossal crowds there, the team had exited for a low display and all had gone well until after canopy deployment. Then, coming in towards the target shortly after opening, many of the team had found themselves no longer masters of their own fate. Whilst their colleagues drifted down to the target as planned, half of the team were seen from the ground to be staying aloft somewhat longer than normal and would clearly be landing as much as a mile off target.

Normal time under the canopy from opening height is in the region of two minutes; yet more than seven minutes after opening there were still parachutes in the sky. Caught in the thermals coming up off the tarmac and rising from the main stands, all they could do was keep going until they were out of the updraft and then head for the nearest shoot-out point. Some tried stalling their canopies to drop through the thermal but such was the lift that was coming up from the ground they remained at the same height; a couple had at one point gained two or three hundred feet whilst under canopy, and they had landed more than a mile from the crosses, almost eight minutes after pulling their ripcords.

That Paris drop seemed to be the start of a whole series of shows that had been disrupted by inclement conditions — unfavourable winds, low cloud and so forth. The month following the Bath Shows had shown a preponderance of low drops. Typical of this was the weekend that brought June to a close, a weekend in which displays were planned at Liverpool, Manchester, Newbury and Brighton.

Chocks were away at Brize on the Saturday morning at 10.20 after loading up the Land Rover and its accompanying trailer with all the equipment and personal effects that the team would be needing over the weekend. The vehicle had been rolled up the ramp and into the belly of the Hercules where it was secured for the flight to Woodford in Manchester. The whole journey was made above thick, billowing clouds that seemed to be covering the whole country at about 3,000 feet. From above, they seemed almost thick and soft enough to lay back in as though in some huge eiderdown. An hour later, after the Herc. had landed at Woodford, they presented a different picture; one of ugly, black, menacing 'clag' down to 1,800 feet.

Everyone went off for an early lunch. Spirits were high despite the doubtful conditions and there was the usual cheerful exchange of insults until the time came to emplane or, in the case of the ground party, to make ready on the DZ.

The drop was due for 2.15 and by one o'clock the Land Rover was in position a few yards in front of the crowd of a hundred thousand plus, and surrounded by helicopters, a Lancaster, Hurricane and assortment of aircraft scheduled to participate in the programme.

Sid released the first balloon and it made off at a rapid rate of knots horizontally across the airfield. At 1,300 feet it disappeared into the clouds. With that combination of wind and cloud, it was going to need another act of God if this jump were to take place.

The Hercules came taxiing along the runway a few yards away and a hand appeared waving out of the window, a brief farewell prior to take-off. Five minutes later, the aircraft was steaming overhead at 1,000 feet for the benefit of the crowd, then it slowly climbed away from the airfield to prepare for the drop.

Meanwhile, the show proper began with a Vulcan on full-power take-off. A more compelling and devastating experience one could hardly have imagined. Sid, Trevor, John Conrad and I were all by the Land Rover as usual, going about their business as the Vulcan began its take-off run three hundred yards up the runway. They were used to aircraft taking off only a matter of yards away and expected a lot of noise. But no-one was prepared for the sheer power and violence of the cacophony that was to follow. Sid was leaning over the runway side of the Land Rover, preoccupied with the laces on his boots, whilst John and Trevor continued taking their readings.

The Vulcan was approaching rapidly and would be lifting off level with the DZ vehicle and only forty to fifty yards away, at which point the engines would be on full power. The noise was surprisingly tolerable as the monster drew level and the ground crew paid it little attention, but Vulcans do not take kindly to being ignored. The great beast lifted its snout as the afterburners were activated and neat fuel was injected into the system. By this time, the Vulcan had gone past and was now giving ground control the full benefit of its power unit at the rear. Sid forgot his bootlaces, taken by surprise, and clapped his hands over his ears in great haste. Come to think of it, that was the fastest Sid had moved for months. John and Trevor too stood with fingers poked firmly in ears with expressions of considerable anguish on their faces and mouthing something like, "Goodness me, what a loud noise!" or, at least, words to that effect, possibly rather less printable than those indicated.

Meanwhile, the act of God that was needed, appeared to be materialising yet again. It was beginning to look slightly more than just coincidence the way that this happened time after time. Ten minutes before P-hour on the final drop instructions from the ground, there was enough sky for a stack pull at 3,300 feet and the wind was down to an easy 6 to 8 knots.

They came out four to five hundred yards late of the flare, falling free for perhaps eight seconds before opening up and spiralling down towards the crosses. Bob Kent was first down, bang on target and hooking round late to turn into wind. Despite his considerable weight and consequent tendency to fall faster than most beneath the canopy, he stood up neatly if a trifle heavily, whilst all around him, his colleagues followed him in. Everybody landed within a circle of perhaps twenty or so yards diameter and the target area suddenly became an extremely crowded place to be.

Dave Ross came in in characteristically extravagant fashion, with a huge grin beneath his bristling and equally extravagant moustache. Always entertaining with outrageous antics beneath the canopy, Dave had both hands off his steering toggles at fifty feet. Instead, he had manoeuvred himself precisely into wind for his landing whilst still above fifty feet, then came down waving cheerfully to the crowd. He stood up on landing, still waving to a delighted and amused audience.

"Come on then, give me a wave," he had invited them at thirty feet and many had obliged. Dave always cut a bit of a dash and was known as one of the team's colourful characters, a fast-talking Scotsman always brimful of energy. Even on the occasions that he consumed more of his favourite brew than was advisable he would go to sleep standing up with only the wall for support.

Seconds after Dave had landed, Joe McCready came in close by for one of the softest and most immaculate landings to date, literally as though he had stepped off a low chair. He bowed an acknowledgement of the crowd's applause and stepped out of his harness to join the line-up. The day's light winds were tailor-made for a parachutist of Joe's light frame and with over a thousand descents behind him his experience showed. Along with Graham Pierce, John Gregor and Bob

Kent, he had been a member of that year's team which had won the four-man speed star National Championships, an event where teams of four compete to put a link together in the minimum possible time.

The drop completed, the team were presented with a plaque in memory of the occasion, another of many that were collected each season. Then they could relax with none of the usual rushing about that frequently followed display jumps. After putting their 'chutes on to the equipment trailer, they took the opportunity to get amongst the crowd to distribute brochures, stickers and badges. Youngsters would occasionally become over-enthusiastic and climb the fence in a quest for autographs whereupon they would promptly get sent back — but they always got the autographs they came in search of.

It transpired that Joe McCready's descent had not been without incident after all. He was sporting a rather bloody chin which had been gashed when it hit the reserve pack after a violent opening. He evidently considered it a minor detail and joined the rest of the team as they went across to the other side of the airfield to repack.

The Woodford Air Display was still in full swing and as the team went about their packing, the Islander of the Army Parachute Display Team, the Red Devils, began circling overhead in preparation for their drop. Today, their luck was out. Conditions really were appalling and the team must have been on the verge of cancelling. Even at minimum drop height on the run in the aircraft was enveloped by ominous black clouds which were scudding across the sky and indicating winds which must have been close to the limit. The team's 'spotter' would probably be sighting the target only intermittently and a fair amount of guesswork would be playing its part.

With a perfect spot, the jump would have been difficult enough; but when the Devils exited at 2,000 feet for a stack pull they were already out of the hunt as far as the target was concerned and faced a long walk across the airfield back to their vehicle. So today was the day that the Falcons made one most forceful point; their drop had been as near a total success as dammit under the circumstances whilst the Devils had soon afterwards, quite frankly, made a hash of it.

Yet parachuting is at best a game of fluctuating fortunes and if the teams had swopped timings on the day, who knows what might have happened? The two teams are, of course, world famous, and there is the same (usually) friendly rivalry between them as between any leading sporting teams and personalities. The Devils are widely respected for their expertise and parachuting knowledge; today, they would have been more than justified in calling the whole thing off, but parachute display teams generally dislike disappointing audiences who have frequently been waiting for hours, and they particularly dislike cancelling at the major shows where there are upwards of fifty to one hundred thousand spectators.

The afternoon was spent in fairly leisurely fashion with a meal on board the parked Hercules and a de-brief of the drop just completed. Some of the team were tending to pull on their own timing rather than on the lowest man's (normally Graham's or Bob's) extractor 'chute, and this was affecting the pattern of the stack in the sky. Others had held off too long, turning their canopies away from the target and into wind in expectation of gusts nearer the ground. The gusts had not materialised which had necessitated a good deal of driving with the wind right up to the last moments before landing in order to get in, a potential cause of an untidy and frequently painful landing.

Then there was the next drop to think about, taking place at an arena known as Wavertree Park in Liverpool in just a couple of hours. There was a lot of poring over the map of the proposed venue, fifteen hundred yards from the Mersey and necessitating the wearing of lifejackets. The local railway station and sidings looked dangerously close, and all round the target the rooftops of terraced houses left frighteningly little room for manoeuvre if anything went wrong.

It was serious faces indeed that studied the DZ photo a short while afterwards as the aircraft circled 2,000 feet above Liverpool ready for the 4.30 P-hour. There seemed to be an atmosphere of thoughtfulness and puzzlement and general concern about this one. Then it became clear why; Bob, and Dave Armstrong had discovered that the DZ photo they had prepared was of a quite different place ten miles away. Bob and Dave had feverishly got to work on the flight deck preparing another photo and wrestling frantically with maps and set squares and the like.

As the team began fitting up above Liverpool with the sun glinting off the Mersey, there appeared to be little sign of any activity on the DZ—in fact it was empty. Presumably, the organisers had changed the venue without letting the team know or there was another arena elsewhere with a similar name.

Suddenly there was visual contact with the arena proper—two miles west of the expected point. More map and photo consultation. Then wind reports coming up from the ground—gusts of 20 knots plus. The time was a testing one and for once, the morale of the team seemed to flag. No one was happy about this one.

"Suddenly that DZ doesn't look so big," Alistair commented as the latest wind figures came over the Tannoy. "If those winds drop out on the way down you land well short." A glance out of the window showed that if that were to happen there was perilously little open space to land short in. The decision on 'go' or 'no go' was Simon's and he got John Conrad on the ground to release another balloon for a final check.

The imperturbable Roger Nicolle was his usual amusing self, wetting a finger and holding it aloft with a puzzled look on his face. "Damn all wind is there? What are we waiting for?" Roger it was who professed to being terrified witless by his early jumps but to look at him now it was hard to believe. He always seemed totally unworried during times of stress and normally bids the aircraft farewell with an enthusiastic grin.

(*Above*) A hazy view of the Bath arena from 12,000 feet, seen from the window in the port door. The fuel tank of the Hercules points the way. (*Below left*) Roger Nicolle half an hour before jumping into Bath arena. (*Below right*) Four minutes to go and most of the team are assembled on the ramp. Impact with the Bath arena is just seven minutes and 12,000 feet away.

Team leader Simon 'bales out' over Bath arena at 12,000 feet, fractionally before his smoke begins to show. Note flap under armpit of jumpsuit, giving lift and extra control.

Rog Nicolle attacks the slipstream at 12,000 feet with customary vigour. Dave Armstrong looks on.

'Up front' on the flight deck. Chris Hayson, surrounded by dials, knobs, levers and switches, looks for canopies in the sky after dropping his cargo.

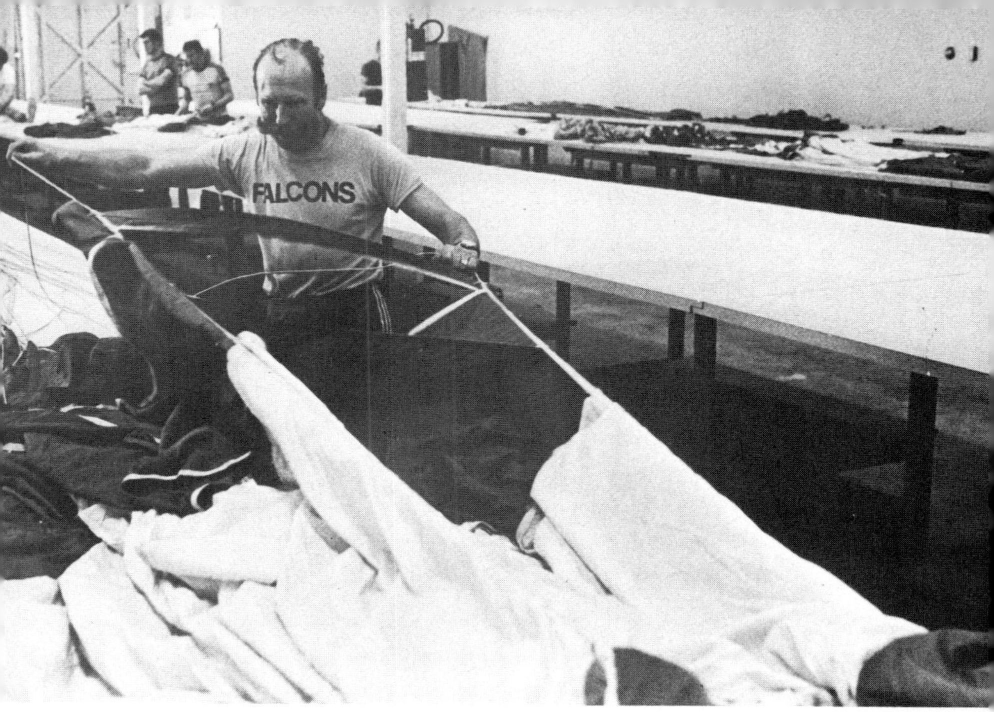

The energetic Dave Ross, busy as ever, sorts a canopy out at R.A.F. Honington ready for the Colchester display.

Dave Ross engrossed in processing of weather data prior to dummy run over Colchester. Notice special headgear with built-in earphones and throat microphone, keeping him and Simon in constant touch with the flight deck.

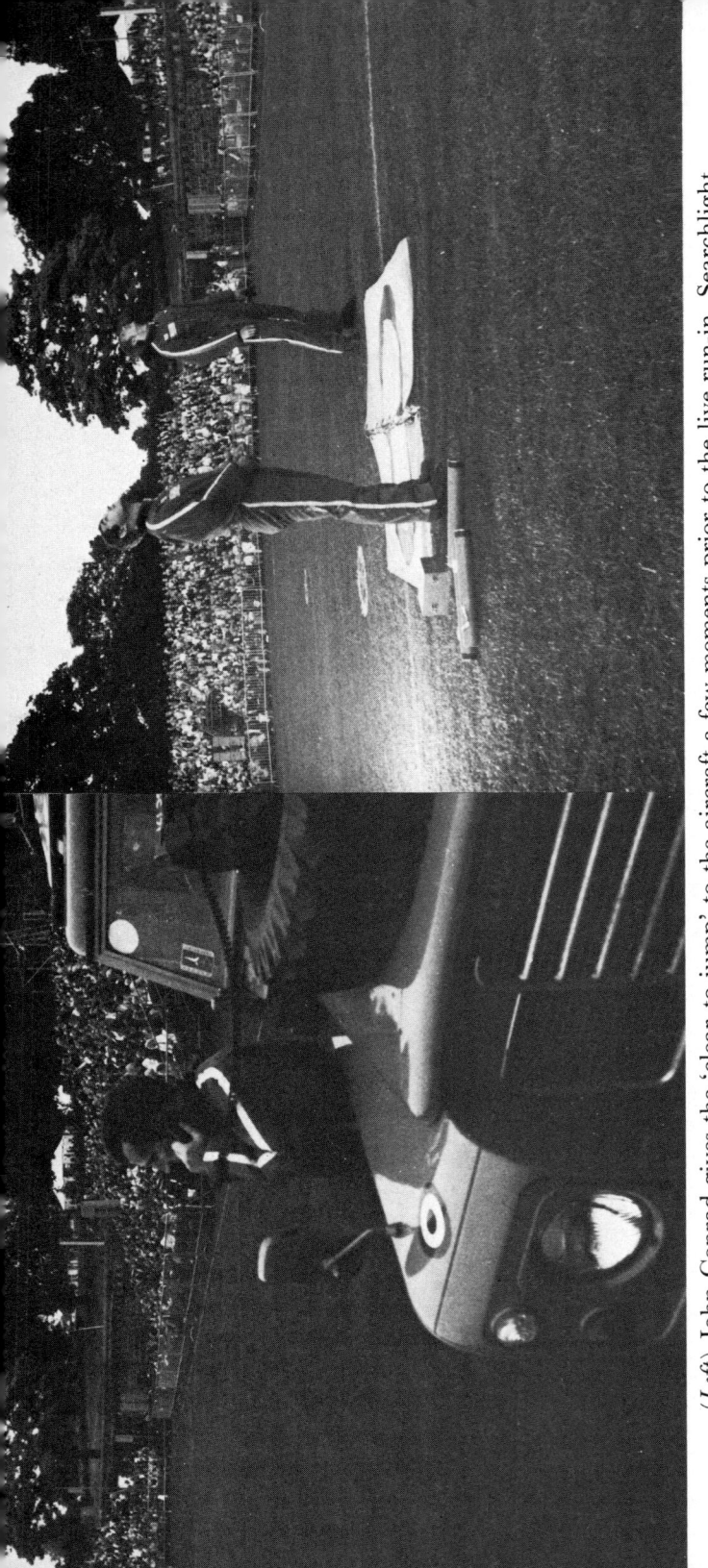

(*Left*) John Conrad gives the 'clear to jump' to the aircraft a few moments prior to the live run-in. Searchlight to his rear, points out the target crosses in the gloom of approaching dusk. (*Right*) Trevor and Sid scour the skies for the approaching Hercules. Notice windspeed markers set at 'o' m.p.h.

(*Left*) John Gregor enjoying the slipstream 12,000 feet over the Colchester Searchlight Tattoo. Graham has gone out before him and is now turning in to link up with Bob Kent for the start of the six-man relative group. (*Centre*) Alistair in classic exit position two miles above Colchester. (*Right*) Dave Ross, last out of the aircraft on the starboard side, smiles a farewell over Colchester. *Top right*, by the door, is the green light indicating 'O.K. for exit'.

Moment of truth for Bob Kent. The very latest of late hooks brings him spinning dizzily into the Colchester arena. The centrifugal force has sent his flag and smoke seven or eight feet above his head.

Falcons' salute. A view from the ramp of the Hercules after the low pass over Colchester arena. Canopies litter the target crosses after the third and, as it transpired, final drop, possibly the finest display performed all season.

Low pass and line up beneath the searchlights of the Colchester Tattoo. Timed to perfection but the DZ flare outstaying its welcome somewhat.

But not today. The latest wind figures were through — surface winds gusting 22 knots. For once, the elements really did not want to know. Simon gave an 'abort' gesture, a slicing motion of the hand at the neck, and whoops of relief rent the air as equipment was removed.

But the excitement wasn't over — not by a long chalk. The people below may have missed the drop but the pilot would try and make up for that with a fast low run and steep climb before turning away. The message went around the aircraft by word of mouth and I looked up from a window at the starboard door to see everyone at the other end of the aircraft diving into seat belts with an uncharacteristic lack of nonchalance.

Steve Rowe shouted somewhat agitatedly, "Get into a seat belt, quick!" We were obviously losing height quickly and increasing speed even more quickly. Not for the first time, I had a helpless and horrifying feeling that something was wrong with the controls or that the pilot had gone haywire. Everyone knew that the Special Forces chaps liked to show a crowd what the Herc. could do and all were aware that one of their number was flying us today.

"Hold on to everything, we're going upside down!" Roger Nicolle was hollering. I looked at him, horrified, and suddenly had the ridiculous thought, "But a Hercules won't fly upside down." It was only then that I realised that both he and Steve were grinning all over their faces. They were about the only ones that were, though. The rest of us were beginning to cringe slightly. The Land Rover and trailer were aboard and one had absurd visions of them breaking free, running back to the tail of the aircraft and stalling it out of the sky.

Buildings and trees were flashing by again as the Herc. hit three hundred miles an hour. At the end of the run, the aircraft was put into a sudden and heart-stopping eighty-degree bank, pulling something in excess of 2g and pinning everyone to their seats. Most of the faces around me contorted in considerable discomfort; it felt almost as though the blood was draining away from the upper body and it seemed an instinctive reaction to squeeze the stomach muscles to restrict the blood flow there. I learned later that this is in fact a technique used by fighter pilots when pulling four or five g in their loops and turns. But that was another story. You would expect to feel strange sensations in a fighter aircraft but few, if any of the team really expected that sort of shock to the system in a bulky and seemingly lumbering troop transporter.

John Gregor had gone up front for the fly past and watched pop-eyed as the port wing suddenly tipped to point straight down to the ground. He was even more agitated to see that the aircraft was not climbing reassuringly on the turn as was usual but was remaining depressingly close to the ground as the power was poured on for the turn. At this point, he confessed to closing his eyes and hanging on for dear life but he was far from being alone in that.

Steve and Roger still seemed to be enjoying the whole affair which tended to lead one to the inescapable conclusion that they were either very hardened flyers or quite, quite mad.

Joe McCready was normally serious and reserved in the aircraft anyway but it was clear that he had not been the slightest bit amused. Many of his colleagues were similarly inclined and cursed the captain roundly. Even the normally imperturbable Dave Ross with his vastness of experience was uneasy. He had been in an Andover crash not many years before in which four Falcons had been killed on take-off. On another occasion, he had been looking out of the port-door window to see the wing touch the ground, without (incredibly) bringing the rest of the plane down. So accidents could and did happen. The pilots were amongst the most professional in the world but they were also human beings and subject to making misjudgements. Yet one knew they were only making the Herc. do what it was safely capable of doing within specified limits.

It may seem strange that a team of top parachutists should dislike the thrills of 'hairy' flying where the pilot himself doesn't give it a second thought. There is one simple and very good reason for that: when the team are jumping, they it is who are in control, who know exactly what they are doing and why. When they are flying, all the control and knowledge is in the hands of the pilot and all his passengers can do is place their complete faith in him. After the Liverpool fly past, even the flight engineer confessed he had been 'feeling it' even though the bulk of his working life was spent at the controls in all manner of flying conditions.

The team flew back to Liverpool, somewhat subdued, to land at Speke Airport where transport was laid on to take them to their hotel. That night, they went their separate ways to a couple of functions where they were honorary guests and, reluctantly, just managed to force themselves to accept their hosts' offers of the evening's drinks on the house.

The next morning, they were back on the coach again to pick up the Herc. waiting at Speke. Take-off was scheduled for 9.30 ready for an 11.30 exit over Newbury for the Greenham Common International Air Tattoo, one of the country's largest annual air displays attracting hordes of visitors each year.

Neither the coach nor the aircraft were the healthiest of places to be that morning, since the previous evening's debauchery was rebounding on all and sundry as the beer fumes rent the air. John Gregor frequently excelled in this department and today was no exception. (So *that* was why he always sat curled up on a seat alone in the corner of the Hercules!) The drinks might have been free the night before but everybody was paying for them now.

Graham Pierce spent most of the flight over to Newbury stretched out along three seats, a customary method of travelling for him. Come to think of it, these days he was pushing Bob Kent hard for the title of horizontal champion. Tommy and Alistair, too, were sleeping it off, feet propped up on the Land Rover trailer. Known as 'The Tartan Trackers', along with Dave Ross, the two had a lot in common, namely their Scottish nationality, their roles in the team and most of all their almost identical senses of humour which tended to spot chinks in people's armour and put them on the defensive. They seemed able to extract humour out of any situation. In fact, most of the team had a very strong humorous streak in their different ways. Pierce with his zany clowning, Gregor with his outrageous stories, Joe McCready with his impressions and jokes, Dave Ross with his bouncy extravagance, Dave Armstrong with his measured and thoughtful dryness, Sid with his (usually) good-natured insults and irreverence, Bob Kent and Rog Nicolle who in their separate ways saw the funny side of everything . . . the diversity of humour was almost endless and it was sometimes like being involved in a travelling circus when everyone was on form.

Approaching P-hour over Greenham, cloud base was down to 5,200 feet. They went out a thousand yards late of the flare, dipping their shoulders left and right in the slipstream as their baggy jumpsuits flared out to give a little more wind resistance to work against. The doors were closed abruptly and everyone quickly got up front for the low pass. Sid, John Conrad and Trevor were still aboard with the Land Rover — they would be landing soon at Greenham to drive to Brighton for the Shoreham Airport display.

"Don't forget to lock your knees," the loadmaster advised as everyone squeezed onto the flight deck. As it happened, it was a moderately civilised fly past this time although a casual R.A.F. observer who had obtained permission to fly on a trip did not take the loadmaster's advice soon enough. It was difficult to suppress a grin when the steep climb came at the end of the run and he sank slowly but irresistibly to his knees, looking up at those around him helplessly with a puzzled look on his face.

Back in the aircraft belly, Trevor was looking ashen. He had decided to stay there where he could stretch out and strap himself in and rest. He had fallen asleep and woken up to see the local trees and houses hurtling by as they normally did on the low pass, but in his sleep-befuddled state he had interpreted this as an indication that the aircraft was 'going in'. The shock to his system went straight to his stomach and he found himself reaching for an air-sickness bag which he promptly threw up into. Just to come down from the flight deck and see him with his head in his hands was enough to start the rest of us off and Trevor soon had company. I had been fighting the urge for half an hour or more and, as we were landing soon, thought I might get away with it.

"As soon as you have to start fighting it, you might as well give up," the loadie chuckled. "Once you reach that stage, you know you've got it coming." Well, I thought, you don't have to sound so cheerful about it. He was right, though. Just as the wheels touched the tarmac the waves of nausea finally overwhelmed me. On reflection, I was quite pleased with that performance; I had held on until at least ten minutes after everyone else.

It was good to get on the ground and in the sunshine ready for the Land Rover trip to Shoreham where the Falcons were due to drop at four o'clock that afternoon. It was a long drive but Sid and Trevor kept the party amused with their cheerful exchange of insults. When the pressure was off, and sometimes when it was on, they and 'J.C.' made an entertaining trio as they worked at the DZ.

At the packed Shoreham Airport in intermittent sunshine, Sid got to work putting the crosses out whilst a Hurricane was putting on a show a few feet above his head.

Right on P-hour, the Hercules began the live run in, restricted now to a 6,000 feet clover leaf display where the first four out would link together and the remainder would track symmetrically in an upwind turn to pull at either 3,000 or 2,500 feet. The four-man link would break at 4,000 and bomb-burst out to the 2,000-foot opening points.

For once, the jump was not all that it might have been. The crowd loved it, that was for sure. But from their own professional standpoint, the team were not happy with it. The tracking had not been symmetrical and the free-fall part of the display had not really demonstrated the clover leaf effect as it was supposed to. It might well have been a straightforward stack pull with a little tracking and relative work thrown in.

The landings, though, had been as entertaining as ever. Graham had stood up on the cross for his first dead centre of the season; Joe had nearly had his canopy incinerated on the DZ flare; Bob Kent had encountered a sudden gust on landing and piled in with great gusto; a similar gust had caught Roger unawares and he found himself, still in good spirits, being dragged across the target area for some seconds. It's difficult to imagine anyone being cheerful under such trying circumstances but as usual Roger was the first to see the funny side of it.

"Ah. I enjoyed that. S'pose I should have capewelled really but it makes such a bloody mess of the canopy," he explained afterwards with his usual grin.

At the briefing immediately after the jump, doubts were beginning to creep in about the value of the clover leaf display pattern, the main problem seeming to be that there was a minimum of time to complete all of the manoeuvres; the tracking times, for example, were too short to show up on the ground as a distinct bomb-bursting effect.

If the truth were known, the bulk of the crowd would probably not have known any different anyway, but Simon would want to get that one sorted out both for his own and the team's satisfaction. Lesser parachute teams sometimes seemed a trifle envious of the Falcons' status; a succession of foul-ups such as failed clover leafs was likely to give the 'antis' ammunition to snipe with.

In the final analysis, the people for whom it all took place cared least that all had not gone perfectly. For all they knew, it had, and as far as they were concerned it was all so much magic and that was what mattered.

An hour of brochure-distributing and autograph-signing amongst the crowd and it was time to assemble by the Land Rover for the journey from the airfield to the hotel ten minutes up the dual carriageway which ran past Shoreham Airport. Since there was a problem with transport, most of the team climbed aboard the show organiser's airfield wagon, an open affair without seats and definitely not designed for carrying a horde of parachutists. When that was packed to capacity, those remaining climbed aboard either the Land Rover roof or the trailer attached to it. In the latter case, Bob Kent and Graham Pierce lounged recklessly on top of the trailer with nothing to hold on to and in imminent danger of being pitched onto the motorway at any moment. It was all highly illegal and most entertaining, particularly when the whole team was waved through the traffic jams like royalty by the local constabulary. They responded by waving regally to their public who were lined along the route to the airport.

The travelling circus arrived at their hotel a few minutes later and piled out noisily. They would rest up here for the night before travelling back to Brize the next morning by coach. Everyone went to their respective rooms to change from sweaty jumpsuits to more relaxed evening wear. Graham, Bob and Dave Armstrong were sharing one of the larger rooms. Bob was horizontal within five minutes. Graham was cleaning his teeth. He turned to Dave. "No putting your teeth in this mug, O.K.?" he warned Dave. Bob had surfaced. "Yes," he agreed, "And no leaving your wig draped over my chair!"

Dave, good-natured as ever and with no need of either of these accessories, laughed as much as anyone at the thought. That sort of humour was typical of the rapport which all of the team had established with each other.

This easy-going nature of internal relationships was probably rather important. It meant that whenever things did not go exactly as planned, nobody was down for long; there was always someone having a laugh or creating one.

That evening, everybody repaired to the local hostelries and thence, later on, to the bar of the hotel which kept 'flexible' hours for residents, and particularly for well-known parachute teams. But by one o'clock, most had had enough and retired to their rooms to 'crash out', shattered, into bed. Graham, however, had become engrossed in a late night darts session and other nefarious activities as was frequently his wont. At 4 a.m., he finally decided to call it a day and staggered to his room where Bob, Dave and, on this occasion myself, were predictably asleep and hoping to stay that way. But Graham had other ideas. Crash! The door flew open. Clump! In he came. Slam! The door was shut. Rattle! Click! On came the table light, flooding the room. "Jesus sodding Christ!" He collapsed, spreadeagled, on to his bed. "What a bloody night." He gazed at the floor for a few moments with his head hanging over the edge of the bed, waiting to elicit some response from his slumbering colleagues. All to no avail, however. They were putting on a tolerably convincing act of being dead to the world. I made the mistake of showing signs of life, though, and for the next half hour received, in detail, an account of the night's debauchery which, dear reader, since this is a respectable book about parachuting, we need not go into.

"Aha!" Dave and Bob agreed the following morning over breakfast, large, knowing grins indicating their familiarity with the eccentric ways of the zany Pierce, "never let on you're awake when he does that; once he starts, you'll never stop him; just keep pretending you're asleep." The information was filed for future reference.

After breakfast, there was time for an hour's lazing in the sun prior to boarding the coach for the drive back to Brize — not as quick as a Herc. and not much more comfortable, but at least it allowed a few hours for collapsing into a seat and catching up on lost sleep until morale was restored to its proper level. It was at times like this that Bob Kent would frequently play a vital role in determining team morale-level; if it was high and the team were feeling in good spirit, Bob it was who would take out his mouth organ and perform an endless string of tunes until morale was back down to a more acceptable level. When morale was really high and everyone was feeling on top of the world, Bob also had an accordion, his playing of which was slightly worse than that of his mouth organ and which consequently was guaranteed to destroy morale totally for the rest of the day. The best way to survive one of Bob's musical sessions on a coach was to try and sleep through it. Consequently, whenever he produced either of the dreaded instruments, colleagues would tend to move to another part of the bus or keel over where they were as though in a dead faint. Bob, ever an individualist, was nevertheless impervious to the insults and doubts cast on his musical talents and would doggedly go through his whole repertoire.

Today, happily, he had brought neither instrument with him and the party was allowed to return to Brize Norton with morale unimpaired.

TWELVE

"Off the Ramp"

The Exeter Display was a beaut. The team had assembled at ten that morning ready for the forty-minute trip over to the West Country. Everyone seemed on a high because the weather was what every parachutist dreams about.

The flight to Exeter was made largely above choked motorways as the teeming holiday traffic crawled painfully along the main holiday routes into Devon and Cornwall. Some of the traffic would be going to the air display and would probably still be snarled up in the queues a couple of hours after the Herc. had landed; sometimes, that aircraft was like a magic carpet, oblivious to crowded roads and all the irritants that go with them, travelling the length or breadth of the country in minutes rather than hours. It landed at the airport little more than half an hour after take off from Brize and everyone strolled out on to the tarmac to stretch their legs, or helped roll the Land Rover and trailer down the ramp ready for the DZ party.

Alistair's hay fever was playing him up again and he sniffed his way through the morning with an inhalant stuffed up his nose for much of the time. It hadn't stifled his aggressive sense of humour, though.

"Nervous smoke, Gregor?" he shouted after John as the latter went across to the Land Rover to get a light. "I don't know how you get so worked up; we're not jumping for another couple of hours!"

Everyone made their way across to the V.I.P. tent for an early lunch and thence to the briefing point on the airfield enclosure, prior to emplaning for the drop to take place immediately after the Red Arrows' curtain raiser. Today, the

Falcons would get their full 12,000 feet; the base and pin would aim to be together by 11,000, and by 8,000 the whole 'relly' group of six would hope to be comfortably docked.

There was the usual fun and games on the DZ beforehand as the Arrows hurtled by a few feet above the Land Rover. Sid, Trevor and J.C. tried to go about their work regardless but were constantly mindful of the incident at an earlier display at Prestwick Airport in which a Starfighter had screamed overhead terrifyingly close to the roof of the DZ vehicle and for some moments they had thought they were for it. He was either a brilliant pilot or had made a near-fatal error; either way, he had nearly added one more to the astonishingly long list of Starfighters to have ploughed in.

John began sending up the weather readings; the team would exit one thousand yards late of the flare to land in ground wind speeds of about 10 knots. For once, Sid was caught on the hop as the Hercules appeared overhead with smoke trailing from the starboard door before he had time to make ready with the flare. It didn't, in the event, prove disastrous. Simon and Dave had probably been spotting with the aid of the crosses and the team appeared in the sky in exactly the right place, steered smoothly in and surrounded the target. Things had become a little hectic and crowded around the impact point, however, and Tommy and Steve had late hooked into the area with the inevitable and painful crash landing. Graham called Trevor across to have a look at his canopy which had been burnt somewhat on his hot smoke container; it would be unserviceable for the rest of that weekend.

Apart from that, everything was spot-on and the team were in an elated mood as they re-emplaned almost immediately for the flight to North Luffenham and the second display of the day. On the ground there, the DZ back-up crew were waiting, since the regular DZ team were at present with their equipment in the Hercules and unable to land at Luffenham. In the aircraft, the whole team was whooping in anticipation of what

139

they hoped would be another 12,000-footer in perfect conditions.

Stan gave Graham a mock fanfare as he made his usual pre-
jump visit to the emergency loo. For once, Graham did
everyone the service of using the in-flight curtain and squatted
contentedly for some minutes, peering round the curtain and
alternately grinning and grimacing. One of life's natural
comedians was Graham when the mood took him.

Simon and Dave Ross were kitted up well before anyone
else; they had a fair amount to do regarding maps and spotting and similar preparatory work and it was impressive to observe the calmness with which they worked as the aircraft got
ever nearer to its destination. Everything was looking good and
the team were looking forward to the drop more than they had
done for many a day.

Rog Nicolle was checking everyone's equipment.

"You can always tell the nervous ones," he confided in mock
seriousness. "I won't mention any names, but sometimes they
join the starboard stick for a check then skip across to the port
stick for a second opinion."

Joe was his usual serious self in the aircraft, checking
everything in minute detail; Alistair sniff, sniff, sniffing under
his hay fever attack as he fitted up his smokes. Then all over to
the doors, there to hang their heads out for a preliminary look
at the target.

Bob Kent was looking incongruously as though he had an
enormous bosom, the front of his jumpsuit stuffed with a
smoke canister attached to the ensign that he would throw out
under the canopy at 1,000 feet.

To a man, they were cool and professional where many
would be gibbering wrecks. Joe pretended to stifle a yawn as
everyone stood poised on the ramp ready to pull their smokes,
much as if to say, "What a crashing bore this all is." That
pretence could hardly have been further from the truth. That
much was obvious from the look of rapt concentration on the
faces of the others as they waited for the thumbs-up. However

good they felt about the jump, the usual tense, heart-pounding expectancy in the moments prior to exit was by far the most overriding impression of the whole exercise. As they went out of the door, it was as though a tap had been turned on to release a great flood of tension; as always, the thinking about it was more nerve wracking than the actual doing of it. Now that they were out, there was no time for worrying about what could or might happen. Everything was 'now' and total commitment to achieving the link up or the bomb burst pattern in the few seconds available.

From the vantage point of the aeroplane, the whole drop appeared to go like a dream until the team disappeared from view and Stan brought the doors down. The impression was confirmed a few moments later as a message came up from the ground thanking the aircrew for their work. All twelve jumpers had glided down effortlessly onto the target. They waved a farewell as the Herc. flew over on a slow pass with the ramp down and the lights on so that the crowd could see inside the belly of the craft. Then they were off, firstly for a meal put on by the organisers, then to take the coach to R.A.F. Waddington, whence the Herc. would be taking off in the morning to take the team to Leeds. For the moment, though, it was flying to R.A.F. Scampton where those still aboard would disembark for another coach to Waddington.

The gathering that evening at Waddington was fairly typical, yet a bit subdued since there was inevitably fatigue from doing two displays in one afternoon. Five of the team hired a taxi to take them out to a local 'do' looking resplendent in blazers and flannels. They returned, mortified and sheepish, soon afterwards. The place had been a centre for the area's motor bike gangs and naturally enough they had felt ludicrously overdressed in the midst of a sea of jeans, tee-shirts and leathers, so had returned to join their colleagues for a mild but prolonged session in the Mess.

Graham Pierce was up to his zany tricks again, seated with his trousers rolled up to the knee, quite as if it were the most natural thing in the world, as a defence against the humid evening air.

The following morning was a relaxed affair; late breakfast followed by a leisurely couple of hours lounging in the sunshine by the aircraft standing by for a 1 p.m. take-off. The Special Forces aircrew joined the team on the airfield. Their usual task was transporting Special Air Service personnel whilst taking the Falcons on displays was more of an ancillary duty, regarded by most of them as fun flying.

After the late breakfast, there was now an early lunch to contend with; that on top of three or four heavy meals from the day before (their own rations plus meals laid on by display organisers) and the considerable quantities of liquor of the preceding evening. One could only pray for a smooth flight or it would be hell up there! It would probably be bad enough anyway with Gregor, so to speak, clearing his system. He had been known to empty a parked coach load of Falcons in approximately five seconds, a feat which he regarded with some pride.

The Herc. left the ground on schedule and set course for the venue, Roundhay Park, climbing steeply to 1,000 feet before dropping the right wing and making for the DZ six miles east of Leeds-Bradford Airport.

For a while, the sky was as clear as a bell, until ten minutes from the venue. Then, at 6,000 feet, a thick, white bank of broken cloud was encountered, a beautiful sight but as far as the drop was concerned an ominous one. So, up to 12,000 and see what the ground looked like from there, whilst the aircrew sought visual contact with the DZ, lining up maps on their knees with the picture two miles below them. The ground was visible through holes in the cloud for perhaps only fifty per cent of the time but enough to find the right release point.

The team donned lifejackets in preparation for the drop (since the park was close to a large lake) then carried on with their usual pre-jump idiosyncrasies; Graham performing his ten-minute squat, John Gregor curled up in the corner seat,

Joe McCready and Phil Kelly quiet and composed as usual,
Simon and Dave Ross preoccupied and workmanlike at the
rear end of the aircraft, Tommy and Alistair sharing an
irreverent joke, Steve Rowe taking great gulps of oxygen, Bob
Kent ready ahead of time, eager for a good, early look at the
target from the door. Roger and Dave Armstrong alone
seemed never to display behavioural quirks prior to jumping.

Up front in the cockpit, the aircrew had spotted the target.
"We'll give you a look at it in one minute," the captain's voice
came over the radio to Simon.

"O.K." Simon returned. "If we get a thick bank of cloud
we'll go round again."

Now there was a constant exchange of information and
checks over the head phones as streams of messages poured
back and forth between the ground, the aircrew and Simon
and Dave Ross.

"Dummy run next time round?" the captain suggested.
Then, "see that speedboat circling in the lake?"

"That's our rescue craft," Simon countered as the rest of the
team clustered round the door. If it had been, they would
barely have been needing it today with a surface wind of 5
knots. Yet the cloud was still there; the team would be hitting
it after twenty or so seconds of free fall and have to hope that it
did not entirely obliterate their view of the target.

John Conrad's voice came over the headset, to the pilot.

"I'm doing a commentary on this one and our dialogue is
being relayed to a few thousand people so be careful what you
say."

"O.K. John," came the reply, "I've got a sore head and don't
feel much like talking anyway."

Then suddenly the small talk had to stop. There was a
problem. The support cable had gone on the port door and no
amount of heaving and straining would lift it clear. Simon had to
think quickly. He had two choices—cancel the jump or use the
ramp on the display for the very first time. There was hardly
a second's hesitation—it had to be the ramp. The spotting

would be more difficult since the forward view from the ramp was restricted, but that could be overcome.

The tailgate began to drop like some great beast opening its jaws as the Herc. lined up on target for the run in. Simon and Dave were on their knees immediately with their heads right out over the side of the tailgate and looking straight into the teeth of the slipstream, the flesh around their mouths and cheeks blown into a contorted and rippling mess.

The rest of the team, for their part, stood apprehensive and elated, facing the ramp for a change instead of standing on it. Jumping off the ramp seemed somehow a far more clinical and cold-blooded way of exiting the aircraft than did leaping out of the doors; it was literally just like stepping off a platform into a huge vacuum, except that that crazy, screaming slipstream would be trying to hurl them about the sky like puppets.

The sudden and last minute change of plan was approached with completely unruffled calm. It took something like two minutes to change from being ready for a door exit to a ramp exit whilst all the time the scream of the slipstream almost obliterated all other noise.

The green light came on to indicate that the target was now directly below. Now it was up to Simon and Dave to decide how long to wait before giving the thumbs up. It wouldn't be long since the winds were low and so, perhaps ten seconds late of the flare, they began the awe-inspiring walk the length of the ramp. On reaching the edge, each man turned to face the way he had come and stepped out and away into space. It was a pretty close-bunched exit and the whole team was out in rather less than the usual five seconds it took to exit from the doors, waving goodbye briefly or grinning animatedly from behind their goggles.

Once their faces had disappeared over the edge, that was the last one was able to see of them; there was no question of peering out of a door to follow their descent as they settled into the track or relative work, since both doors were closed.

Leaning over the edge of the tailgate for a better view was both perilous and 'verboten' particularly in view of the fact that there had been no time to attach a safety harness to a strong point in the aircraft.

The next time the team were in sight from the aircraft, they were in one immaculate line of fourteen with Simon at the front taking the salute. From the way their canopies had hidden the crosses and surrounding target area from view, they had all obviously hit the target with consummate ease. In fact, one was to learn later, the furthest relative worker had been five feet from the cross and the trackers not much more. As the Herc. passed overhead for the second time, on a slow run with the ramp still down, they waved their thanks to the aircrew whilst the crowd of perhaps forty thousand surrounded the team enthusiastically.

Back at Leeds-Bradford Airport later, where the team returned to by coach from the venue in order to re-board the aircraft for the trip back to Brize, it soon became clear just how spectacular the drop had been. Exiting the ramp at 12,000, the team had, as expected, hit patchy cloud at 7,000 and fallen stable through it down to 5,000. Until then, they had only been visible intermittently from the ground through gaps in the cloud, but as they cleared the layer of cloud they suddenly and dramatically shot into the blue, bomb-bursting outwards and tracking at maximum speed for possibly the best display effect they had ever performed. The audience in the arena were ecstatic and the team were in danger of being mobbed as people surged forward with well-meaning words of congratulation but unaware that precious canopies were being trampled underfoot. It was often the case at the small shows where the Falcons were the only major attraction. Security would be less stringent and the informal, intimate atmosphere of a park or playing field rather than an R.A.F. airfield always tended to make a crowd demonstrate its excitement and enthusiasm more.

The organisers had laid on the beers, of course, and the

team had relaxed at the park for an hour or so before getting back on the road again to pick up the plane. Here, another meal was waiting which they set about with customary vigour. Then it was 'chocks away' again and a flight back to Brize at bumpy, low altitude which most were too tired to notice, but sat shaking and rocking back and forth in sleep as the tireless Stan continued to stride about energetically performing the various tasks of loadmaster. Where flying about the countryside tended to shatter most people, Stan appeared to thrive on it and he rarely flagged; a sort of direct opposite to Bob Kent and Graham Pierce who were stretched now along a couple of seats, their heads resting on the canopies they had used earlier in the day. The horizontal champions were flat out again.

THIRTEEN

The Big One

There were tight drop zones and easy drop zones, hazardous ones and doddles; but the drop zone at the East of England Show in Peterborough was, from a jumper's point of view, one of the very worst. It consisted of the smallest of arenas, oval in shape, with a maximum usable length of perhaps seventy-five yards and width not much more than half that. Little enough room for error there, even were everything else ideal. But additionally, and completely encircling the arena, was a ring of thirty-foot flag poles and judging by the way the flags were flapping at the top, the wind was out to do its worst.

Along the length of the west side of the arena ran the main grandstand, a thirty-foot high impenetrable barrier providing a roof for two thousand spectators. The prevailing wind would mean that the team would be coming into the arena directly over that roof and with a windspeed over 20 knots at 1,000 feet, they would be motoring.

The projected time for P-hour was critical. The show had to keep to a strict schedule of events and as the ground party drove into the arena to set up the DZ, show jumping fences were still being removed with the Herc. starting its run in just a couple of minutes away. Sid and Trevor dashed about putting crosses and flares into position to the accompaniment of the commentator's voice informing the crowd of the approach of "the foremost parachute display team in the world".

The aircraft passed overhead, and for a while it seemed that this run had merely been a dummy one, such was the distance that it overflew the target. Then, fully 2,000 yards late of the flare, the team popped out at 7,000 feet for the start of the clover leaf display pattern. It was strange to see those familiar smoke trails so far away from the target and even stranger to see that the team was really still only a group of dots even after they had been under canopy for some thirty seconds.

From the centre of that arena, there seemed to be no way that any of the team would get anywhere near the target. The general feeling on the ground was that they might as well forget the display, throw the show away and look for a safe undershoot. But what those on the ground had not allowed for was the fact that, with the team being so far away on opening, it was difficult to appreciate the speed with which they were now driving in towards the target. The powerful following wind and the natural drive of the Para-Commander would probably be combining to give an approach speed in the region of thirty-five miles an hour at 1,000 feet.

Thirty seconds before impact, the best part of a mile had been made up under the canopy and it began to look as though the front runners were in with a chance of making the arena. Moments later, they came soaring over the main stand, running hard with the wind perhaps forty or fifty feet above the roof, scanning the ground earnestly. The turn into wind would be critical if the landing were to be a painless one.

It must have been a strange spectacle for the spectators beneath the roof of the stand; they would have seen nothing of the free fall and very little of the canopy travel. For them, the first view of the display was a pair of legs appearing over the edge of the roof, to drop suddenly into the small patch of green in front of them followed by a body as frequently as not crumpling into a dishevelled heap on the ground.

With the first men in, it began to look as though the last few to exit the aircraft would follow suit although their passage over the roof was always an anxiety-fraught exercise. One or two seemed perilously close to the building, almost needing to lift their feet to clear it safely. Either way, there were few stand-up landings today. The approach to the target was the ideal set up for the late hook in that they had to turn into wind late, and close to the ground, as soon as the roof had been cleared. The immediate result was a sudden loss of height and in most cases a moment of high drama as they impacted with a vengeance.

It didn't bother Tommy, of course, even though the crowd did let out a gasp of surprise as he piled in. That was standard procedure for him but this time everybody actually heard the landing, a sort of dull, crumpling thud that would have prostrated most men. Tommy may have had more hard landings than most but he certainly knew how to do it and get away with it.

John Gregor had been first down and the rest hard on his heels, swinging in low over the roof to turn sharply into wind at the last moment.

On that showing, their introduction to the crowd as the world's number one parachute display team could hardly be denied; it had been by far the most impressive and professional show they had put on all summer. As the commentator had pointed out, the fact that all of the team were top athletes in their own right in certain fields enabled them to pull out that little bit extra when the really demanding displays came along. Indeed, a glance at the list of specialities within the team reveals highly competent gymnasts, canoeists, skiers, mountaineers, skin divers, trampolinists as well as those with representative honours in the major games. Yet despite, or possibly because of the wealth of talent within the group there was never any blowing of one's own trumpet, just an enormous and unspoken confidence in their own and each other's ability.

This basic and natural athleticism was perhaps the fundamental reason they had been able to go thus far through the season with so few injuries. Alistair was currently limping painfully about with an acute sprain, the result of an unhappy landing at the Southampton Show the previous week in which everyone had apparently 'hit the ground' rather than landed. Happily, they had all walked away from that one, apart from Ali who had been stretchered off the DZ with an ankle twice its normal size. In reality, that was perhaps a tolerable price to pay for many months of continuous jumping in all manner of conditions and places. At least he was able to laugh about it as he limped his way about dragging the delinquent foot behind him. Whenever the team set off to go anywhere by foot, he would set out a few minutes earlier to avoid getting left behind. If the truth were known, it was probably breaking his heart to be missing out on special descents such as the one that had just been completed.

That evening in the bar at R.A.F. Wittering, there was the usual get-together that followed most displays. Wittering was a five-minute drive from the showground and was therefore a natural stop-over place for the second display on the following day. There was the usual good-natured banter and a few recent team photographs were being passed round. They were large, tolerably clear prints but when they were passed over to Tommy for perusal, he scanned the first two or three briefly then made the customary 'abort' signal, slicing his fingers across his throat.

"It's no good. I can't make head or tail of these," he confided with a grin and shake of the head. He got a blank look in response.

"It's true," a colleague confirmed generously. "Silly old sod's as blind as a bat. Can't see his hand in front of his face."

That explained a lot — mainly Tommy's tendency to give people heart attacks with his late hooks coming into land. There was something at once both comic and heroic about this ace parachutist hammering flamboyantly into drop zones all over the country, invariably hitting the target with unerring accuracy, albeit a trifle heavily, whilst at the same time being hard pressed to make visual sense of a ten by eight photograph. Rumour had it that he never bothered to use an altimeter but on a 12,000 foot drop would count slowly from one to sixty before pulling. One of life's natural characters was Tommy.

That was one great thing about the Falcons. They had more

than their share of characters and each year tended to throw up more. Consequently, their life style sometimes gave the impression of being one long round of parachuting thrills followed by frequent evenings of making merry in whatever place of entertainment was at hand — an impression that was not always too far from the truth. After the pressures of important and often highly emotionally taxing display jumps, the natural desire was to relax and unwind and have a laugh and a drink. There was seldom any shortage of either of those two commodities and there were some hilarious moments which would live in everybody's memory. Like the time when the highly respectable Dave Ross let his hair down, as he occasionally did, and decided to sample the wines of Paris on the team's annual visit to the air show there. The evening culminated in Dave directing the teeming traffic of Paris, stationing himself perilously in the centre of the main carriageway and spinning round in an alcoholic haze as speeding cars and hooting taxis roared past. On such evenings of abandonment, it was not unusual for Dave to end up fast asleep standing up. On one memorable occasion, he got through a complete hot dog without opening his eyes once, the bristling handlebar moustache working up and down furiously as he devoured the prize.

Then there was the time Gregsy got legless and had to get up in the night for a widdle, at which point he mistook the wardrobe door for that leading to the loo and a hapless room mate's boots were never quite the same again. Worse had been known. The doughty 'Drossy' (as Dave Ross was nicknamed for obvious reasons) had, in one of his more stupendous moments, made a similar mis-assumption with regard to a chest of drawers, only for a slightly less mentionable purpose than a mere widdle. There was an unwritten law on the team that those guilty of such horrendous misdemeanours be banished for the rest of that night to solitary confinement elsewhere.

The Peterborough jump safely over, it was time to move on again, this time to Great Yarmouth where the team ran out of the good luck which had attended them thus far into the season. The nature of the target area with its curtain of obstacles to be cleared meant that all of the team had to turn into wind late and low, the classic late hook situation inevitably leading to some interesting landings. Everyone piled in. Some got away with it, notably Tommy for whom it was standard procedure and who therefore had something of an unfair advantage over the others! But Phil Kelly collected a couple of broken toes for his trouble; John Gregor came out of it with both badly-bruised feet being taped up and Steve Rowe brought out the ambulance with an agonisingly dislocated elbow and injured arm. That made a total of four out of action for the Finningley drop a few days later, at which show the Queen would be reviewing the Royal Air Force.

Reinforcements were called in; Henry MacDonald, gymnast and highly experienced jumper from the 1971 Falcons team, and Terry Cooke, another gymnast who had completed his three year stint on the team the season before. That brought the numbers up to ten, and on the Wednesday prior to the Friday Royal Review, those ten exited the Herc. at 3,500 feet above Finningley airfield. It was by way of a final rehearsal but at that comparatively low height a ten-man stack pull had to suffice.

It was a strange descent, full of incident. Roger, one of the last to leave the aircraft, pulled his ripcord as soon as he saw the low man's drogue 'chute appear, then settled back into a comfortable spread in anticipation of the reassuring jerk of his own canopy. For an uncomfortably long time, nothing happened and Roger found himself dropping way below the rest of the team. His drogue was 'burbling' in the partial vacuum his falling body was leaving behind it. It should have cleared itself quite quickly in the normal course of events but for five or six hundred feet continued to flap uselessly on his back without coming clear of the pack. Roger didn't have a lot of height to play with. His hand instinctively went to the reserve handle, yet something told him to hesitate a fraction longer before pulling. What if the main 'chute finally did come clear just as the reserve was deploying? Entanglements in those sort of situations have in the past caused fatalities. At least if the main had gone up and turned out to be 'a bundle of washing' he could have cut away from it and ensured a clean reserve deployment. Roger took one final look above his head. Still nothing there. Right! The reserve it would have to be. His hand clenched around the handle protruding from the side of the reserve on his belly and he prepared to whip over on to his back to allow the reserve canopy to come out cleanly. Then suddenly there was a loud crack and a harsh tug at the shoulders. The main 'chute had at last come good at something like 1,200 feet. It was as well that the reserve handle had stayed in its pocket.

Predictably, Roger landed long before anyone else despite his position of penultimate jumper out of the aircraft. In contrast to the drama of a minute before, he landed softly just feet short of the cross, before Bob, Graham and Dave Armstrong came in hard on each other's heels to do stand ups a similar distance away.

The normally foxy Dave Ross had for once been caught unawares; he came in thirty seconds behind the main group, obviously trapped in a thermal and taken possibly sixty yards beyond the target with no way back in.

Joe, too, was in a thermal, an unusually powerful one by the looks of things. At 800 feet, he just seemed to hang and hang in the air and make no progress whatsoever. At one point, he most definitely went up! Understandably, he didn't even try to run back for the line up but stayed where he had landed, about three hundred yards away, to roll up his 'chute.

Henry MacDonald, similarly light of frame as was Joe, seemed to be caught in the same thermal and was working to drive out of it, stall out of it or lose height by any other means open to him. But he was taken a good hundred yards beyond the cross and had to sprint back to make the line up as the Herc. made its low pass.

The season's normal quota of problems were beginning to make themselves felt at the wrong time. What was perhaps the most important venue of the year was imminent. A full five days were to be spent jumping into the tiny arena of the Colchester Tattoo, possibly the most difficult and potentially dangerous DZ the team would tackle all summer, but definitely the most atmospherically electrifying show they would perform in any one year. In a way, the Colchester Tattoo was the climax of the season and any jump performed after it would seem easy in comparison. The arena itself was in something of a bowl and surrounded by tiered seats, commentary box, tall trees and scaffolding. In short, it was a display parachutist's nightmare. Most teams would not take the job on. Those who had invariably came a cropper. Without a doubt, this was the big one.

Everything was scheduled precisely to the minute from the opening fanfare to the finale; this would be the ultimate test of the Falcons' display organisation and a measure of the professionalism that had been built up as a result of the display campaign of recent months.

The first jump into the arena would be by way of a dress rehearsal on the Tuesday at sunset, and as the fanfares sounded a dramatic introduction to the show, conditions were nigh perfect. Four Phantoms screamed low over the arena, the evening sunshine glinting softly on the sleek wings. A buzz of excitement passed through the crowd of whom tonight there were perhaps no more than four thousand, although that number would swell to six or seven thousand later in the week for the 'official' shows. Yet that small crowd always generated infinitely more atmosphere than the hundreds of thousands at shows like Biggin Hill or Paris ever did. The large airfields were usually detached, cold and uninviting; here, there was the intimacy of a genuinely warm welcome from an appreciative audience. It was as though they instinctively felt that this drop was something special; that where many drops were routine in comparison, this one had too much of an element of danger, or at least of calculated risk, to ignore.

Down on the DZ, John, Sid and Trevor joked to conceal their apprehension and wondered how the hell Tommy was going to see that tiny target area from the air. There would be no smoke or flare until less than a minute from P-hour since the DZ vehicle would not be able to enter the arena before then. That was how critical the timing was and it would necessitate Simon and Dave spotting with the aid of the adjacent funfair which could be seen from 12,000 feet where the green of the arena was quite invisible.

Ten minutes before the drop, everyone piled into the Land Rover ready to drive up to the main door leading into the arena.

"Got the keys, boss?" Sid asked John as they sat waiting to depart. "Keys? I thought you had them," John replied. Sid began fumbling frantically through his pockets. "Christ! I haven't got them. Where the hell are they?" He disappeared round the back of the Land Rover, flushed and agitated, to see if he had dropped them there. John sat looking straight ahead at the arena doors which would swing open in about thirty seconds time, leaving the DZ party and Land Rover exposed to four thousand pairs of eyes. If those keys weren't found quickly, there would be the humbling experience of being stranded in a non-startable vehicle with four thousand people waiting expectantly for it to be driven into the arena. It was rather like one of those dreams when you suddenly find yourself naked in a busy street.

Sid returned, all pockets and zips as he fished about in his jumpsuit for the keys. Trevor cursed Sid quietly, but then there was nothing unusual about that; Trevor was always cursing Sid quietly. Sid suddenly grinned triumphantly and hoisted the keys aloft.

The doors swung open and the Land Rover sprinted in with Trevor and Sid standing on the steps at the side and clinging on to the roof rack, ready for a rapid dismount. Each was dropped off at his prearranged point clutching crosses, flares,

anemometer, wind speed indicator and the like, whilst John
sped off to tuck the vehicle away in a corner of the arena where
it would be less likely to constitute a hazard. Like magic, the
aircraft appeared overhead immediately, homing in on the
flare 12,000 feet below.

The wind was almost non-existent and the aircraft was
perhaps only one or two hundred yards late of the flare when
eleven smoke-trailing dots appeared in the sky. Steve and Phil
were still unfit and not jumping. John Gregor and Alistair
were up there, though, despite considerable pain from their
recent argument with the ground. John's toes were giving him
some stick but he had told the doc that it was the heels which
were hurting and the doc had given him the O.K. to jump.
Terry Cooke was in again to make the numbers up to eleven.

The atmosphere was charged with anticipation. The buzz of
excitement which passed through the crowd as soon as the aircraft appeared changed to a roar as the smoke trails of the
team began to show. That roar increased steadily as the dots at
the head of the smoke trails gradually turned into recognisable
shapes, the body positions clear now in a flawless evening sky.
In fact, the activity up there was so clear now it felt almost as
though the whole team had decided to pull low. The four-man
relative group had got together early and a fifth could be seen
fighting his way in; Joe McCready was pulling out all the stops,
trying to fly through the burble created by the other four.
Someone had him by one arm and he was in briefly before, as
one man, the group turned outwards and tracked away to
open up.

Meanwhile, to the right of the relly group, two of the
trackers appeared to be heading straight towards each other at
what would be a closing speed of perhaps one hundred and
forty miles an hour. In fact, they were probably at different
heights such that there were hundreds of feet between them,
but from the ground it made one cringe to think of the shud-
dering impact such a collision would bring. One would have
sworn that they hurtled past each other with inches to spare,

but optical illusions can play some weird and wonderful tricks in those situations. In this case, what had happened was that two of the trackers had completed the usual outward and inward bomb-burst only to find that they were falling towards an opening point too close to the arena. They therefore turned back again in an outward track at a time when the remainder of the trackers were completing the inward track, but since they had their own area of sky to work in, the manoeuvre presented no problems.

It was strange to think that those tiny figures so far above the arena were scanning the ground, searching and studying the earth as they fell, like great birds of prey seeking out the next victim. Yet from the ground it was impossible to equate how such a fall looked with how it actually felt to perform that fall. No one on the ground could possibly feel the tension and heady excitement of the seconds before leaving the aircraft; nor could they hear the formidable howling of the slipstream, feel that slipstream wrapping cold and powerful arms around them, the cacophonic rush of air at terminal velocity; they could never know the dizzy approach of the earth as it began to rush towards them as the time came to pull, neither could they feel the taut, pulling jerk of the 'chute's opening and biting pressure of the leg straps and harness as they took up the strain.

Yet, for all that, merely to watch the proceedings was spectacular and exhilarating in the extreme if the reaction of the crowd was anything to go by. As the first canopies opened, the wild cheering of the crowd would hardly have disgraced the winning goal at Wembley. It continued all the way to the ground, the noise funnelling upwards from the natural 'bowl' of the arena such that the team could hear it as soon as their parachutes were open. Then, as they descended, so the noise became progressively more pronounced until, at the moment of impact, they were enveloped by a crescendo of applause.

It was easy to see why the Tattoo was considered the high point of the season. There was no doubt who were the stars at this show, especially when they all came down on a sixpence as they did tonight. It all looked so easy and effortless — too easy perhaps? The next two or three days would decide. For the moment, though, it was time to stow 'chutes away in the trailer whence they would be recovered the following day for re-packing.

John and Ali were still limping grimly as the team assembled at the Land Rover parked now outside the arena, but one was led to understand that this was nothing that a bit of alcoholic physiotherapy couldn't put right. So, into the town to find a suitable establishment; not normally a difficult thing to do since most of the team have an in-built radar device which homes in on just such places. In fact, possessing this rare talent is one of the prime qualifications for getting on to the team and by the time the average three-year tour on the team is over, the talent has usually been honed and tuned to a fine and exquisite art.

The place chosen had both one-armed bandit and dart board, so Graham was immediately in his element, secreting himself in a corner and indulging his love of the bandit before taking over the dart board for a session with the locals. By the following evening, the whole team would be regarded as 'locals' themselves, such was the impact with which they would 'hit' a place and, in the nicest possible way, take it over. There was never any trouble, no-one ever became objectionable or out of hand, or too busy or preoccupied to sign autographs; in short, most evenings away were a public relations exercise in themselves. There were no angels on the team, that was for sure, but there were no villains either . . . well, not many anyway!

The following evening was the first show 'proper'. ATV had their cameras positioned both in the air and on the ground. Again, the winds were almost nil and conditions more or less perfect as P-hour (8.30) approached, the sun's last rays begin-ning to disappear over the horizon. Yet 12,000 feet above the arena, the aircraft was still in strong, direct sunlight and shone like a beacon where those in the arena were beginning to feel the chill of dusk.

Again, the sky was gin-clear — except for one small block of cloud which lay directly above the arena at 11,000 feet. At 8.30 precisely, the Hercules disappeared behind that cloud. At 8.30 and 20 seconds, the Falcons appeared, screaming out of the cloud and into the blue, evening air, into the view of a spellbound six thousand people. The trackers were already well into their max. track with their smoke spewing and billowing from their feet as they rocketed out of the cloud. The relative group, on the other hand, were as close together as they could normally expect to be at that height (10,000 feet) even were there no cloud at all. But to get together so soon when 'working-time' had been disastrously curtailed by a thousand foot thickness of cloud was some achievement. By 9,500 feet, they had it made; the five-man link was complete and flying stable, steady as a rock. "Jesus Christ, look at that five-man," John Conrad muttered as he stood with the DZ vehicle keeping the pilot up to date with the situation. The five were falling almost directly above the arena; Bob, Graham, John, Joe and latest addition Terry Cooke who was obviously already well and truly at home with his new team mates. He was the ideal man for the job, having won the four-man speed star National Championships along with the other four the year before.

Tonight, the link was so early and good that no-one wanted to let it go and they held on to that five-man just as long as they possibly could. It did not matter that their whoops of exhilaration could be heard neither by each other nor by those on the ground; it was enough to see the looks on each other's faces to know that this one was special; it mattered not that their combined cries of delight were lost on the wind as the link was ridden down to 4,000 feet. At this point, Graham would normally give the nod and the group would break up and track away to open. Tonight, he held on as the four faces gazing steadfastly at him, waiting for the nod, started to become wide-eyed with expectancy as the group went through 4,000 feet.

Meanwhile, on the ground, the five were now almost as large as life itself, their combined smokes forming a single thick column behind them. There were cries from the crowd. "Look at the middle five holding hands," one woman, who was quite carried away, shouted excitedly. It hardly seemed the time to tell her that they were not in fact holding hands but clinging onto the sleeves of each other's jumpsuits. In any case, the people she was directing the advice to hardly needed it; the circle stood out so well that they could not have missed it. Every bend in every limb was as clear as if they were just feet away. Then, where before the five had seemed almost to be floating on the air, they appeared suddenly to be looming larger by the second; it was time to pull. Almost lazily, they bent at the waist to turn away and began the brief outward track, plummeting like bricks now, before flaring out to get maximum lift and therefore minimum speed, which in turn would allow a less violent opening.

For once, the whole of the pull could be seen in detail. Normally, it was a confused hotchpotch of arms and legs. In this evening's perfect viewing conditions, a ground observer could clearly see the right arm coming in for the ripcord, an action which inevitably sends any parachutist on to his back or head down unless he compensates with the left arm for loss of lift from the right arm. Quite how that compensation is achieved was there for all to see tonight, the left moving forward and reaching out in front of the helmet to give lift to the upper body and prevent the natural tendency to go head down.

Eleven canopies opened safely as usual, followed two or three seconds later by a succession of 'Cr-a-a-cks' as the sound filtered down from two and three thousand feet. As on the first drop, finding the crosses was easy. Simon's spotting had come on by leaps and bounds over the months and it was evidently an art which he had now mastered. On a tight show like Colchester, the spot was half the battle and there was little doubt that all of the team would be stomping the crosses on the second drop as they had on the first. The only problem was that the lack of any wind in the arena inevitably meant a few hard landings, particularly when everyone was coming in hard on each other's heels and would be unable to manoeuvre exactly as they would have wished.

They could live with that, though, especially with the crescendo of applause that accompanied their landings acting as an anaesthetic.

The third and what turned out to be final night, however, was rather less of a doddle than the first two had been. In fact, it was quite simply the most difficult display jump many of the team had ever undertaken. The main problem was the upper winds, gusting over 20 knots, with next to nothing on the ground. Those sort of eccentric wind readings were rarely consistent or reliable and likely to change by the minute. But John Conrad had little choice but to send up the figures that his instruments gave him and Simon similarly little choice but to accept them.

So it was that on the third descent, on the Thursday evening, the team popped out over Colchester more than a mile from the arena. In the almost total calm of the arena, it was hard to see how they were ever going to make up that distance. As in the Peterborough arena, and as in all late releases into small venues, there was the curious deception that they were just too far away. But that upper wind was good and true and driving all eleven canopies in at perhaps thirty miles an hour; and suddenly, they were over the arena, driving in hard to set themselves up for the crosses before the wind dropped out at fifty feet. And drop out it most certainly did. Once inside the bowl, there was nothing to work against; that, combined with the necessity to hook round late from the congestion at fifty feet, resulted in a few pile-ups.

Bob came off worst. His landing must have been audible all round the arena and an involuntary "Oo-oo-oh" erupted from the crowd as they winced in sympathy. He had hooked just a shade too late and dropped like a stone from twenty feet, a shock enough to poleaxe most men, but Bob was fairly used to hard knocks. With his thirteen and a half stone, he had to be. All the same, this one shook him up a little and he was quiet and pale for some minutes afterwards and limping painfully.

Rog Nicolle had looked as though he might do the same thing, turning round to face the main stand perhaps thirty feet from the ground. He began to plummet, much as Bob had done, until with a deft and frantic juggling act with the toggles, he regained full lift about ten feet from the ground and did a stand up without even bending at the knees.

There was the usual delirium from the crowd as the team completed the line up and ran out of the arena waving. Someone said they saw Bob hopping out of the arena waving but one couldn't swear as to the truth of that.

A show like that needed celebrating and everyone went off to do just that at the local. It was one of the rowdier nights and the landlord probably trebled his take that night. Tommy's singing voice was on form whilst John Gregor became involved with the local villains and emerged from the snuggery with packets of cigarettes stuffed into his tracksuit trousers. Later, a packet was found to be missing and he was ready to tear the culprit limb from limb; Graham couldn't resist the opportunity and hinted that he may or may not have the missing packet, taunting John that he did indeed have a pack in his pocket but was not prepared to say what sort.

"Lemme see 'em. I want to see 'em," John insisted.

"Nope." Graham was adamant, but with a mischievous glint in his eye. The episode continued for some minutes until John was convinced that Graham had the cigarettes. Then Graham suddenly produced the packet that he had — the wrong sort. John was mortified to think that he had misjudged his man, offended Graham even.

"All right. I'm sorry. I take it all back. It was all my mistake," he admitted gracefully.

Graham retired to his corner, chuckling gleefully. He

probably had the missing packet secreted about his person elsewhere anyway!

The 'evening' came to a close marginally before dawn, but everyone was up and about again by ten the following morning. John Conrad dragged Tommy out of bed for a game of tennis about which Tommy was rather less than enthusiastic but went through the motions, to give colourful descriptions later of forehand smashes that had disappeared out of court or failed to connect altogether.

Gregsy began the day with his customary flair, naked and larger than life, holding up his trousers and foraging about in the pockets.

"This is the bit I don't like about nights out," he said matter-of-factly, "checking how much money you've got the next morning!"

Bob's first port of call that morning was the hospital. He was back a couple of hours later with his ankle heavily strapped up—nothing broken but severe swelling and sprain. He could scarcely walk on it let alone jump on it. Ali was out of action too. He had had a soft enough landing the previous evening but it had been enough to aggravate a recent injury. That meant only nine men jumping that night.

The nine need not have worried. Fifteen minutes before P-hour, a sudden squall blew up out of a dead calm and clouds rolled overhead at 3,000 feet.

Up in the aircraft, the team were having one of the worst low-level flights they had known. The Herc. was lunging suddenly earthward every few seconds, caught in air pockets below the cloud base. The startling and abrupt loss of 200 feet at a time was hardly increasing the desire to stay inside the aircraft. Simon and Dave were clinging on desperately in the doorways as they spotted, with the very real threat over their heads of being pitched into the slipstream.

Whilst he was in the door, Simon received word from John Conrad of the latest wind figures. Reluctantly, he turned to the team on the ramp, sliced his fingers across his throat and aborted. He received in return a silent and malevolent glare. The bitter disappointment was almost painful and the team tramped disconsolately from the ramp and back to the seats to take their gear off, throw their 'chutes into a corner somewhere and eat their hearts out. Drops like Colchester were really what being on the Falcons was all about, a kind of ultimate in display jumping; it hurt to let down an audience who were so appreciative. Yet Simon had little or no choice but to abort. The light had deteriorated badly, the wind readings were totally unreliable because they were so erratic and John had suggested 'scrubbing' the show when the trees around the arena had started swaying just prior to P-hour.

The Falcons were down on the Tattoo programme to make two more descents the following day, Saturday. There was to be an afternoon drop and the usual evening drop. Sadly, it was not to be. The team never saw Colchester from the air again that year. Friday evening's squall was still around for the whole of the following day and the aircraft did not even leave the ground.

Yet the visit had been memorable for the first three days alone — thirty-three parachutes in the sky, thirty-three parachutists on the crosses. That was going to take some beating. Future teams of Falcons might better the record but it was doubtful if other than they would match it.

Conclusion

And so to the future. The current season was approaching the final run-in after months of hard, continuous display and training jumps. The team was due for a hard-earned period of leave when most would try to forget all about aeroplanes and parachutes for a few weeks and spend some time with their wives and families.

Some would be leaving the team soon to move on to pastures new. Simon would make way for Roger to take over as 'Boss'; Roger, in turn, would have a different team flight sergeant assisting him, possibly the able and experienced Henry Mac-Donald. Dave Ross was in his seventh season with the Falcons and was looking forward to a less intensive role in the world of parachuting. John Conrad, too, would be moving on. Trevor and Sid, however, would in all probability still be on the ground the following year, giving the drop zone boss a hard time and cursing the buggeration factors that would undoubtedly occur again.

Bob, Graham and Steve would be completing their third and final seasons with the Falcons and their humour and experience would be missed. In some ways, it would be a sad parting of the ways, yet there would be fresh faces the following year, new personalities and characters who would make their own impact. Some would be inexperienced in display parachuting but in a remarkably few months would be transformed into the seasoned professionals which were currently in the team and preparing to move out. For the following year's team would undoubtedly show a transformation just as this one had. Recent jumps particularly had been in a different class to those only a few short months earlier when the team were still trying to put the show together over Salisbury Plain and Weston, fighting to overcome the early and inevitable pitfalls. The same problems would occur again next year but there was a lot of talent and expertise at hand to put that right. Joe would be on his way to fifteen hundred jumps during his final season the following year—that was a formidable amount of experience to fall back on when things weren't working out well for the first-year jumpers in training. Then there would be the likes of John Gregor, Dave Armstrong, Phil Kelly, Tommy and Alistair, with the wealth of experience the present season had given them. Those few months of solid jumping were worth five years of most parachutists' lives.

And so one was left to wish the Falcons well for future years and bid a reluctant farewell—reluctant because the last six months had been spent amongst a cheerful, humorous and human group of people who lived by doing what they loved to do and spread a lot of happiness whilst they were doing it.

Perhaps there is a message there for us all.

Index

Index